# EFL Grammar
# for Japanese Students
# and Teachers

**Taeko Kamimura**

Senshu University Press

**EFL Grammar for Japanese Students and Teachers**

**Taeko Kamimura**

ISBN978-4-88125-341-0

Published and distributed by Senshu University Press, Tokyo, Japan.
FAX +81-3-3263-4288

This research was supported by JSPS KAKENHI Grant Number JP15K02698
This publication was funded by a publication grant from Senshu University in 2019.

# Acknowledgments

I would like to thank various people who supported me in conducting this research. Dr. Yutaka Ishii and his research fellows kindly helped me collect data both for high school students and university teachers. Yu Hashimoto helped me to not only design a grammar test and a survey but also analyze the data for the three studies. Sho Kumazawa supported me in analyzing the data for Study 3. Gaku Uehara read the earlier version of the manuscript carefully and gave me helpful suggestions. Mitali Das carefully read the manuscript and gave me detailed, constructive feedback. I would like to thank Dr. Takeshi Takizawa, who initially designed this study with me but passed away before the study was completed. Without his support the study would have never finished. I would also like to thank the participants in the studies, namely, the junior high school and high school teachers and the students at Senshu University and Senshu University High School who kindly provided me with valuable data. Lastly, I am grateful to Emiko Mashimo, who kindly gave me suggestions and edited the manuscript of this book.

# Contents

# Chapter 1

# Introduction

## 1. Introduction

### 1.1 Renewed interest in teaching and learning EFL grammar

Teaching grammar was long deemphasized as a major factor that prevented EFL (English as a Foreign Language) students from developing oral and aural skills in Japan. During the 1990s and 2000s, as a strong reaction to the traditional Grammar-Translation Method, in EFL classrooms at the secondary level in Japan, fluency in spoken English was emphasized more than grammatical accuracy in written English (Hidai et al., 2012). However, the importance of teaching grammar has recently been reconsidered. Otsu (2012), for instance, claimed that, unlike acquiring a first language, students could not acquire a foreign language without learning the grammar of that foreign language. This applies especially to Japanese EFL students who learn English in a context where they have limited exposure to English as a target language. Therefore, Otsu maintained that Japanese EFL students needed to be aware of how the English language was structured and that EFL teachers had to help their learners to raise this awareness.

The argument as made by Otsu (2012) does not mean that we

should go back to the traditional way of teaching grammar, which was represented by the Grammar-Translation Method. Instead, it means that EFL learners and instructors should begin to have a renewed interest in EFL learners' grammatical competence in order to make effective use of grammar for communication as one of the important components of communicative competence (Canale & Swain, 1980).

## 1.2 Past studies in teaching and learning EFL grammar in Japan

Several researchers conducted studies in which the grammatical competence of Japanese students at the secondary-school level was investigated. Kimura and Kanatani (2006), for instance, found that Japanese junior high school students had difficulty with noun phrases, especially those postmodified by prepositional phrases (e.g., "my house in Brazil"). Furthermore, Kimura, Kanatani, and Kobayashi (2010) presented similar findings and argued that a considerable amount of time was needed for Japanese learners to acquire this grammatical construction. Kawamura and Shirahata (2013) gave Japanese high school students a grammar test that included questions on different grammatical items that the students had been taught in English classrooms in junior high school. The analysis of the test scores showed that the students performed best on pronoun questions and worst on participles; the scores on the to-infinities, comparatives, present perfect, passive voice, and relative pronouns were found to be in between. Kamimura (2016) also analyzed high school students' accuracy scores on a grammar test that included sentence structures chosen from a high school textbook on writing. She found several grammatical items on which the high school students scored low, and therefore, she called those "late-acquired" items. Those items included inanimate subjects, relative clauses, comparatives, participles, and the SVOC sentence pattern.

Studies that examined Japanese university EFL students' grammatical competence were also conducted. Nakai (2008) attempted to identify which grammatical items caused problems for university students in remedial classes and found that the students had difficulty with even such basic grammatical structures as the SVOO sentence pattern and interrogative structure. Nakai (2011) further found that another group of students in remedial classes failed to provide correct answers for questions involving complements, present participles, and past participles.

All the studies reviewed above focused on specific grammatical items. Hashimoto and Kamimura (2015) and Hashimoto (2016) prepared a comprehensive grammar test, which included a wider range of grammatical items taught at junior high school and high school in Japan, by referring to *The Course of Study for Junior High Schools, Foreign Languages* (2008) and *The Course of Study for High Schools, Foreign Languages, English* (2010), the guidelines for English education in Japan compiled by the Ministry of Education, Culture, Sports, Science and Technology (MEXT). It was found that what caused serious trouble for Japanese university EFL students were "advanced" items, which were taught in high school, such as the nonrestrictive use of relative adverbs and pronouns, participial construction, and subjunctive past perfect.

From a slightly different angle, Hidai et al. (2012) conducted a survey that examined Japanese EFL students' levels of "understanding" rather than their levels of "difficulty" with various grammatical items. That is, Hidai et al. investigated how the students perceived their understanding of 66 grammatical items chosen from those taught in junior high school and high school. The students answered that they understood most of these items at the sufficient level. When their perceived understanding levels were compared with those of teachers, it was found that the students' perceived understanding levels were considerably higher than the teachers' levels, which suggests that the students overestimated their level of grammatical competence. The greatest gap between the students' and teachers' perceptions was clearly observed in the complex sentence structure.

## 1.3 What needs to be investigated

The studies reviewed above revealed three major findings:

1) There are several grammatical items that Japanese EFL students at the secondary level have difficulties with, such as the noun phrases followed by postmodifiers for junior high students, and participles, inanimate subjects, and relative clauses for high school students;
2) There are several grammatical items that cause problems for Japanese university EFL students, such as the SVOO sentence pattern, relative adverbs and pronouns, participial construction, and the subjunctive past perfect; and
3) Japanese EFL students tend to overestimate their level of understanding of different grammatical items, especially the complex sentence structure.

Concerning teaching and learning EFL grammar in Japan, we still have many areas that need to be investigated. In the following chapters, three studies are reported upon, each attempting to answer the following different research questions:

1) What relationships can be observed between the accuracy rates and difficulty levels of different grammatical items for Japanese EFL university students? (Study 1);
2) Are Japanese EFL students' and teachers' perceived difficulty levels for various grammatical items different from each other? (Study 2); and
3) What are the developmental stages of Japanese EFL students' grammatical competence? (Study 3).

To answer these research questions, three studies (Studies 1, 2, and 3) were conducted. The following chapters report on the findings of those studies.

## 2. Participants

The studies involved three groups of participants. The first group consisted of Japanese university EFL students. They were first-year students who majored in English at a four-year university in Japan. The second group comprised Japanese EFL teachers who taught either at high school or university. The third group was made up of Japanese first-year high school EFL students who were learning English at the high school affiliated to the university that the first group attended. The details of each of group will be explained in subsequent chapters.

## 3. Data collection

In this section, a grammar test prepared for students and a survey prepared for teachers will be explained. The grammar test was used in all the three studies, whereas the questionnaire accompanying the test was used in Studies 1 and 2. Table 1.1 shows the design of the grammar tests for the university and high school students and of the questionnaire for the teachers.

### 3.1 Grammar test and questionnaire

#### 3.1.1 Grammar test for university EFL students

Past studies, such as those by Kawamura and Sirahata (2013), Kawamura (2014), and Nakai (2008), focused on specific

**Table 1.1**  *Design of the Grammar Test and Questionnaire*

|  | Part | Section | University students | High school students | Teachers |
|---|---|---|---|---|---|
| Grammar test | Part 1 | Section 1 | 23 | 34 | Question-naire 110 |
| | | Section 2 | 32 | | |
| | Part 2 | Section 1 | 23 | 42 | |
| | | Section 2 | 32 | | |

grammar items. In the present studies, however, a more comprehensive grammar test was prepared, following Hashimoto and Kamimura (2015) and Hashimoto (2016).

The test consisted of 110 questions, each of which was targeted at a different grammatical item, as shown in Table 1.2. The test was comprehensive enough to cover all the grammatical items included in *The Course of Study for Junior High Schools, Foreign Languages* (2008) and *The Course of Study for High Schools, Foreign Languages, English* (2010), which were compiled as guidelines for English education by the Japanese Ministry of Education, Culture, Sports, Science and Technology. Most of the questions on the test were made by using sample sentences displayed for the various items listed in these guidelines. Seventy-six questions were made by referring to *The Course of Study for Junior High Schools, Foreign Languages* (2008), whereas the remaining 34 questions were made by consulting *The Course of Study for High Schools, Foreign Languages, English* (2010).

The test consisted of two parts, and the Japanese university EFL students as participants took them within a two-week interval. Each part contained 55 questions and was further divided into two subsections. For each question in both subsections, a Japanese sentence was given, and the students were told to make an English sentence that corresponded to the meaning of the Japanese sentence. The first subsection in each part of the test dealt with sentence structures such as those that asked about the simple, compound, and complex sentences as well as the SV, SVC, and SVO sentence patterns. In answering each question in this subsection, the students were told to unscramble the words or phrases given to make an appropriate English sentence. On the other hand, in answering each of the questions in the second subsection, the students were required to fill in the blanks to complete the English sentence that had the same meaning as the Japanese sentence given. Appendix A displays the grammar test for the university students, which was divided into two parts, with a total of 110 questions.

### 3.1.2 Questionnaire for Japanese EFL teachers

A questionnaire was prepared for Japanese EFL teachers to assess the difficulty levels of each grammatical item incorporated into the grammar test that the students took. Appendix B illustrates the questionnaire, where a question, an answer to the question, and a target grammatical item are all shown.

### 3.1.3 Grammar test for Japanese high school students

Appendix C shows the grammar test for high school students, which included a total of 76 questions. Those questions covered the grammatical items listed in *The Course of Study for Junior High Schools, Foreign Languages* (MEXT, 2008). In other words, the test did not include those items listed in *The Course of Study for High Schools, Foreign Languages, English* (MEXT, 2010) because the first-year high school participants had not learnt them yet.

**Table 1.2** *110 Different Grammatical Items Used as Targets in the Questions on the Grammar Tests*

| No. | Target grammatical items | Lists on the Course of Study | Question number on the test for the university students | Question number on the test for the high school students | Question types | Answers |
|---|---|---|---|---|---|---|
| 1 | Simple sentence | | 1-5 | 1-4 | | My teacher will come to my house this afternoon. |
| 2 | Compound sentence | | 1-13 | 1-10 | | Tom went to the supermarket, and his wife stayed home. |
| 3 | Complex sentence | | 2-19 | 1-31 | | I didn't go out because it was raining. |
| 4 | Positive declarative sentence | | 1-9 | 1-7 | Rearranging words into the correct order | Bill has three cats. |
| 5 | Negative declarative sentence | Junior High School | 2-5 | 1-21 | | Emi doesn't like baseball. |
| 6 | Imperative (affirmative) (general verb) | | 1-23 | 1-17 | | Walk slowly, please. |
| 7 | Positive imperative sentence (be verb) | | 2-8 | 1-23 | | Please be quiet, Kenji. |
| 8 | Negative imperative sentence (general verb) | | 1-17 | 1-13 | | Don't run here. |
| 9 | Negative imperative sentence (be verb) | | 2-16 | 1-29 | | Don't be noisy, Erika. |
| 10 | Yes / no question (general verb) | | 1-16 | 1-12 | | Do you walk to school? |

| No. | Target grammatical items | Lists on the Course of Study | Question number on the test for the university students | Question number on the test for the high school students | Question types | Answers |
|-----|--------------------------|------------------------------|--------------------------------------------------------|----------------------------------------------------------|----------------|---------|
| 11 | Yes / no question (be verb) | | 1-4 | 1-3 | | Is this your classroom? |
| 12 | Affirmative question | | 1-2 | 1-2 | | Does she like Japanese food or Chinese food? |
| 13 | Wh-question | | 1-1 | 1-1 | | What did you have for breakfast this morning? |
| 14 | SV | | 1-7 | 1-5 | | He goes to the library by bus when it rains. |
| 15 | SVC (V=be verb) (C=noun) | | 1-20 | 1-15 | | This is my teacher. |
| 16 | SVC (V=be verb) (C=pronoun) | | 2-7 | 1-22 | | The pen on the desk is mine. |
| 17 | SVC (V=be verb) (C=adjective) | | 2-9 | 1-24 | | This game is exciting. |
| 18 | SVC (V=general verb) (C=noun) | | 2-11 | 1-25 | | The girl became a pianist. |
| 19 | SVC (V=general verb) (C=adjective) | | 2-2 | 1-19 | | You look nice in that jacket. |
| 20 | SVO (O=noun) | | 1-8 | 1-6 | | He studies English very hard. |
| 21 | SVO (O=pronoun) | | 1-21 | 1-16 | | Yuko met him yesterday. |
| 22 | SVO (O=gerund) | | 2-21 | 1-33 | Rear-ranging words into the correct order | We like eating the school lunch. |
| 23 | SVO (O=to-infinitive) | | 1-15 | 1-11 | | He hoped to be a doctor. |
| 24 | SVO (O=how to-infinitive) | Junior High School | 2-4 | 1-20 | | My grandfather knows how to use the computer. |
| 25 | SVO (O=that-clause) | | 1-11 | 1-8 | | We didn't know that she was ill. |
| 26 | SVO (O=what-clause) | | 2-23 | 1-34 | | I don't know what he will do next. |
| 27 | S+V+indirect object+direct object (noun) | | 2-17 | 1-30 | | The teacher told us an interesting story. |
| 28 | S+V+indirect object+direct object (pronoun) | | 1-12 | 1-9 | | I will show her that. |
| 29 | S+V+indirect object+direct object (how to-infinitive) | | 2-12 | 1-26 | | I taught him how to send e-mail. |
| 30 | SVOC (C=noun) | | 2-20 | 1-32 | | We call him Ken. |
| 31 | SVOC (C=adjective) | | 1-19 | 1-14 | | You should keep this room clean. |
| 32 | There+be-verb ~ | | 2-15 | 1-28 | | There is an old tree in front of my house. |
| 33 | It+be-verb+(for ~)+to-infinitive | | 2-1 | 1-18 | | It is not easy for me to understand English. |
| 34 | S+tell, want+O+to-infinitive | | 2-13 | 1-27 | | Mary wants you to eat this chocolate. |
| 35 | Personal pronoun (subjective, possessive, objective) | | 1-24 | 2-1 | Fill in the blanks | I saw your parents at the supermarket, and Tom saw them at the station. |
| 36 | Personal, demonstrative pronoun | | 2-26 | 2-24 | | This is my bag, but that one is yours. |

| No. | Target grammatical items | Lists on the Course of Study | Question number on the test for the university students | Question number on the test for the high school students | Question types | Answers |
|---|---|---|---|---|---|---|
| 37 | Pronoun ('some') | | 1-27 | 2-4 | | Some of my friends came to my house. |
| 38 | Relative pronoun ('that' as subject) (restrictive use) | | 1-44 | 2-21 | | Yuki bought a doll that had large beautiful eyes. |
| 39 | Relative pronoun ('which' as object) (restrictive use) | | 2-24 | 2-22 | | This is the dog which I like the best. |
| 40 | Present tense (be verb) | | 1-43 | 2-20 | | We are tired and sleepy. |
| 41 | Present tense (general verb) | | 1-42 | 2-19 | | We take a walk in the park every morning. |
| 42 | Past tense (be verb) | | 2-38 | 2-36 | | He was in China last year. |
| 43 | Past tense (general verb) | | 1-26 | 2-3 | | We watched TV in class today. |
| 44 | Past tense (irregular verb) | | 2-43 | 2-41 | | We swam in the ocean last summer. |
| 45 | Present progressive | | 1-39 | 2-16 | | My mother is talking on the phone. |
| 46 | Past progressive | | 2-42 | 2-40 | | I was reading a book then. |
| 47 | Present perfect (duration) | | 2-25 | 2-23 | | He has lived in London for two years. |
| 48 | Present perfect (experience) | | 1-28 | 2-5 | | I have played this game more than twenty times. |
| 49 | Present perfect (completion) | Junior High School | 2-37 | 2-35 | Fill in the blanks | I have just cleaned my room. |
| 50 | Auxiliary verb (will) (future) | | 1-25 | 2-2 | | It will be fine tomorrow. |
| 51 | Comparative (adjective) (as ~ as) (as tall as) | | 2-34 | 2-32 | | I am as tall as John. |
| 52 | Comparative (adjective) (-er) | | 1-35 | 2-12 | | Ken is taller than Yumi. |
| 53 | Superlative (adjective) (-est) | | 2-27 | 2-25 | | John is the tallest boy in the class. |
| 54 | Comparative (adjective) (as ~ as) (as beautiful as) | | 2-44 | 2-42 | | Tokyo Skytree is as beautiful as Tokyo Tower. |
| 55 | Comparative (adjective) (more+adjective) | | 1-40 | 2-17 | | This picture is more beautiful than that picture. |
| 56 | Superlative (adjective) (most + adjective) | | 2-30 | 2-28 | | Mt. Fuji is the most beautiful mountain in Japan. |
| 57 | Comparative (adjective) (as ~ as) (as good as) | | 1-32 | 2-9 | | This watch is as good as that gold one. |
| 58 | Comparative (adjective) (irregular) | | 1-41 | 2-18 | | This car is better than that red one. |
| 59 | Superlative (adjective) (irregular) | | 2-33 | 2-31 | | This is the best camera in this store. |
| 60 | Comparative (adverb) (as ~ as) (as fast as) | | 1-29 | 2-6 | | Nancy can walk as fast as her sister. |
| 61 | Comparative (adverb) (-er) | | 2-29 | 2-27 | | Jimmy can swim faster than his brother. |
| 62 | Superlative (adverb) (-est) | | 1-34 | 2-11 | | Bolt can run fastest in the world. |

| No. | Target grammatical items | Lists on the Course of Study | Question number on the test for the university students | Question number on the test for the high school students | Question types | Answers |
|---|---|---|---|---|---|---|
| 63 | Comparative (adverb) (as ~ as) (as slowly as) | Junior High School | 2-36 | 2-34 | Fill in the blanks | He drives as slowly as his father. |
| 64 | Comparative (adverb) (more + adverb) | | 2-40 | 2-38 | | Jiro speaks more slowly than Hanako. |
| 65 | Superlative (most+adverb) | | 2-35 | 2-33 | | He eats the most slowly in my family. |
| 66 | Comparative (adverb ) (as ~ as) (as well as) | | 1-36 | 2-13 | | Yumi can play the piano as well as Taro. |
| 67 | Comparative (adverb) (irregular) | | 2-41 | 2-39 | | I like blue better than red. |
| 68 | Superlative (adverb) (irregular) | | 1-31 | 2-8 | | Yoko can play the violin the best in Japan. |
| 69 | To-infinitive (as noun) | | 2-32 | 2-30 | | I want to use English in my future job. |
| 70 | To-infinitive (as adjective) | | 1-38 | 2-15 | | The students had a lot of homework to do. |
| 71 | To-infinitive (as adverb) | | 1-30 | 2-7 | | They went to the supermarket to buy some food. |
| 72 | Gerund (as object) | | 1-33 | 2-10 | | We enjoyed playing tennis. |
| 73 | Present participle (as adjective) (pre-modification) | | 2-28 | 2-26 | | Look at that sleeping baby. |
| 74 | Past participle (as adjective) (post-modification) | | 2-39 | 2-37 | | This is a book read by a lot of students. |
| 75 | Passive voice (present) | | 2-31 | 2-29 | | Judo is enjoyed by many people in the world. |
| 76 | Passive voice (past) | | 1-37 | 2-14 | | This machine was made in France. |
| 77 | SVC (V=general verb) (C=present participle) | High School | 1-3 | | Rear-ranging words into the correct order | I kept working in a Japanese company. |
| 78 | SVC (V = general verb) (C = past participle) | | 2-3 | | | The old man sat surrounded by children. |
| 79 | SVO (O=if-clause) | | 1-6 | | | I wonder if you are free today. |
| 80 | S+V+indirect object+direct object (that-clause) | | 1-10 | | | She told me that she had been busy. |
| 81 | S+V+indirect object+direct object (what-clause) | | 1-14 | | | Please tell me what you want. |
| 82 | S+V+indirect object+direct object (how-clause) | | 2-6 | | | He asked me how I felt. |
| 83 | S+V+indirect object+direct object (if-clause) | | 2-10 | | | I asked her if she was free. |
| 84 | SVOC (C=participle) | | 2-14 | | | I saw the man crossing the road. |
| 85 | SVOC (V = causative verb) (C = bare infinitive) | | 1-18 | | | My father made me wait outside. |
| 86 | SVOC (V = sensory verb) (C = bare infinitive) | | 2-18 | | | I saw a lot of people enter the concert hall. |

| No. | Target grammatical items | Lists on the Course of Study | Question number on the test for the university students | Question number on the test for the high school students | Question types | Answers |
|---|---|---|---|---|---|---|
| 87 | S+seem+to-infinitive | | 1-22 | | Rear-ranging words into the correct order | He seems to be a real adventurer. |
| 88 | It+seems+that-clause | | 2-22 | | | It seems that she is very happy. |
| 89 | Bare infinitive | | 2-47 | | | The teacher let us go home early. |
| 90 | Relative pronoun ('what') | | 1-53 | | | What is important is to put your heart into your music. |
| 91 | Relative pronoun ('who' as nonrestrictive use) | | 1-46 | | | They had a daughter, who went to Europe to study music. |
| 92 | Relative adverb ('where') | | 2-45 | | | This is the house where I lived 30 years ago. |
| 93 | Relative adverb ('when') | | 2-55 | | | I remember the day when we first met. |
| 94 | Relative adverb ('why') | | 2-53 | | | He tries to tell us the reason why trust is important. |
| 95 | Relative adverb ('how') | | 1-51 | | | Do you know how Charles came to school? |
| 96 | Relative adverb ('where' as nonrestrictive use) | | 1-48 | | | She traveled to Seoul, where she met her future husband. |
| 97 | Relative adverb ('when' as nonrestrictive use) | | 1-55 | | | Let's go to Hokkaido in June, when the weather is beautiful. |
| 98 | Auxiliary verb (past) | High School | 2-50 | | Fill in the blanks | When the economy went down, they could not find jobs. |
| 99 | Passive voice and modal auxiliary verb | | 2-54 | | | In clear weather, Mt. Fuji can be seen from Shinjuku. |
| 100 | Modal auxiliary verb and perfective aspect | | 1-52 | | | She must have been extremely angry. |
| 101 | Formal subject (that-clause) | | 1-45 | | | It is important that we read this book. |
| 102 | Formal object (to-infinitive) | | 2-46 | | | I found it easy to solve the problem. |
| 103 | Formal object (that-clause) | | 2-52 | | | I found it strange that Bill went there alone. |
| 104 | Prsent perfect progressive | | 1-47 | | | He has been using the Internet for three hours. |
| 105 | Past perfect | | 2-51 | | | She had lived in London for 10 years before she came back to Japan. |
| 106 | Subjunctive mood (past) | | 2-49 | | | If I knew her number, I would call her. |
| 107 | Subjunctive mood (past) (I wish ~) | | 2-48 | | | I wish I had a new bike. |
| 108 | Subjunctive mood (past perfect) | | 1-54 | | | If I had had enough money, I would have bought a better computer. |
| 109 | Participial construction (action continuing) | | 1-49 | | | I was reading a book on the train, listening to music. |
| 110 | Participial construction (reason) | | 1-50 | | | Having a cold, I had to stay in bed. |
| Notes | | | "1-5" means Question 5 in Part 1. | | | Underlined parts correspond to blanks provided in the questions. |

## 3.2 Questionnaire for students

A questionnaire to investigate the students' perceived level of difficulty for each question was incorporated into the grammar test. Whenever the students answered each question, they were asked to score the difficulty level of answering the question on a six-point Likert scale, where one signified "very easy" and six, "very difficult." Figure 1.1 shows an example of a question with a perceived difficulty scale on the test.

```
健は由美よりも背が高いです。        very easy ⟷ very difficult
Ken (                    ) Yumi.   1  2  3  4  5  6
Expected answer: Ken (is taller than) Yumi.
```

**Figure 1.1**  An example of questions used in the grammar test.

## 3.3 Questionnaire for teachers

A questionnaire was prepared for the teachers as participants based on the grammar test given to the students. On the survey sheet, both the expected answer and target grammatical item for each question were shown. The teachers were asked to surmise and assess the level of difficulty that their students would have when answering each question on the test. Figure 1.2 displays an example of a question and a difficulty scale used in the survey. The questionnaire actually distributed to the teachers is displayed in Appendix B.

```
健は由美よりも背が高いです。        very easy ⟷ very difficult
Ken (                    ) Yumi.   1  2  3  4  5  6
Expected answer: Ken (is taller than) Yumi.
Target grammatical item: Comparative (adjective) (-er)
```

**Figure 1.2**  An example of a question and a difficulty scale used in the survey.

# Chapter 2

*Study 1*

# Japanese university EFL students' accuracy rates and difficulty levels of different grammatical items

## 1. Introduction

Several studies have attempted to identify in which grammatical items Japanese EFL students tended to make errors. Kimura and Kanatani (2006), and Kimura, Kanatani, and Kobayashi (2010), for example, found that Japanese junior high school students demonstrated poor performance on the use of noun phrases followed by prepositional phrases as postmodifiers. Kawamura and Shirahata (2013) also conducted a study which revealed that Japanese high school students scored highest on pronouns and lowest on participles. Chujo, Yokota, Hasegawa, and Nishigaki (2012) examined Japanese university students' performance on their grammar test, finding that the students made errors in questions that involved such items as the subjunctive mood, concessions, and inanimate subjects.

While those studies focused on the students' performance on different grammar tests, Hidai et al. (2012) investigated what they called "the comprehension levels" of various grammatical items both from the students' and teachers' points of view. These levels tried to capture how well the students themselves thought they comprehended each item on the scale from one to four (where one was the lowest and four was the highest score), and also how teachers viewed the comprehension ability of their own students.

Results showed that the students reported that they sufficiently comprehended the majority of the grammatical items investigated, whereas the teachers considered their students as failing to comprehend almost half of the items at a sufficient level. This study was pioneering in that it attempted to measure the comprehension level of many different grammatical items; however, it did not cover all the grammatical items listed in *The Courses of Study for Junior High Schools, Foreign Languages* (MEXT, 2008) and *The Course of Study for High Schools, Foreign Languages, English* (MEXT, 2010). Therefore, a more comprehensive study that deals with a wider range of grammatical structures is called for.

## 2. Purpose of Study 1

The purpose of the present study was to identify grammatical items that are especially problematic for Japanese EFL students in terms of accuracy rates and difficulty levels. Specifically, the following three research questions were posed.

1) Which grammatical items do students regard as easy to answer, but answer incorrectly?
2) Which grammatical items do students regard as difficult, and answer incorrectly?
3) What are the error patterns for the items identified in 1) and 2)?

## 3. Procedure

### 3.1 Participants

Thirty Japanese EFL university students participated in Study 1. They were first-year English majors at a four-year university in Japan. Their English proficiency was considered to be at the low-intermediate level, with an average TOEIC® (Listening and Reading) score of 320.67 points.

## 3.2 Data collection

The students answered each question on the grammar test and the questionnaire as explained in Chapter 1. The test consisted of two parts, each of which had 55 questions that targeted different grammatical items. The students took each part of the test for 35 minutes. The questions were constructed using example sentences shown for the different grammatical items listed in the guidelines for English education in Japan compiled by the Ministry of Education, Culture, Sports, Science and Technology. Seventy-six questions were made by referring to *The Course of Study for Junior High Schools, Foreign Languages* (MEXT, 2008), whereas the remaining 34 questions were made by consulting *The Course of Study for High Schools, Foreign Languages, English* (MEXT, 2010).

Figure 2.1 shows an example of a question used in the grammar test. The students were instructed to fill in the blanks to complete an English sentence that corresponded to the Japanese sentence. They were also told to assess how difficult it was to answer each question using a Likert scale, with one being very easy and six being very difficult.

---

健は由美よりも背が高いです。            very easy ⟷ very difficult
Ken (                    ) Yumi.   1  2  3  4  5  6
Expected answer: Ken (is taller than) Yumi.

---

***Figure 2.1***   An example of a question used in the grammar test.

## 3.3 Data analysis

### 3.3.1 Correct-answer rates

The correct-answer rate for each question was first calculated. Following Brown (1973), Krashen (1977), and Kamimura and Hashimoto (2015), 80% accuracy was set as the threshold level to determine whether or not a given grammatical item had been acquired. The 110 questions were then divided into two categories: (1) items whose accuracy rates were equal to or above 80% and (2) those whose accuracy rates were below 80%.

### 3.3.2 Perceived difficulty levels

The students' average perceived difficulty level was calculated for each grammatical item. The items were again classified into two groups according to the difficulty levels: (1) items for which the students' average difficulty levels were equal to or above four points and (2) those for which their average difficulty levels were equal to or below three points.

### 3.3.3 Classification scheme

A classification scheme was devised by combining the classifications of correct-answer rates and perceived difficulty levels explained above. Figure 2.2 illustrates this scheme, consisting of four groups.

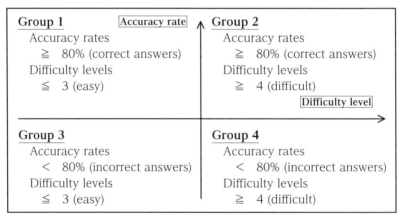

***Figure 2.2*** Classification of grammatical items according to accuracy rates and difficulty levels.

Group 1 includes grammatical items that the students regarded as easy to answer and answered correctly. Group 2 contains items that they regarded as difficult to answer but answered correctly. Group 3 consists of items that they considered easy to answer but answered incorrectly. Finally, Group 4 comprised the items that they perceived to be difficult to answer and also answered incorrectly. To answer the research questions, the present study focused on Group 3 and Group 4.

# 4. Results and discussion

## 4.1 Accuracy rates and difficulty levels

Table 2.1 displays the accuracy rates and difficulty levels for the 110 questions.

**Table 2.1**   *The Accuracy Rates and Difficulty Levels for the 110 Questions*

| No. | Target grammatical items | Accuracy rates | Perceived difficulty levels |
|---|---|---|---|
| 1 | Simple sentence | 96.67% | 1.87 |
| 2 | Compound sentence | 93.33% | 2.57 |
| 3 | Complex sentence | 100.00% | 2.30 |
| 4 | Positive declarative sentence | 100.00% | 1.57 |
| 5 | Negative declarative sentence | 100.00% | 2.00 |
| 6 | Imperative (affirmative) (general verb) | 70.00% | 2.67 |
| 7 | Positive imperative sentence (be verb) | 100.00% | 2.53 |
| 8 | Negative imperative sentence (general verb) | 100.00% | 1.83 |
| 9 | Negative imperative sentence (be verb) | 100.00% | 2.40 |
| 10 | Yes / no question (general verb) | 100.00% | 2.10 |
| 11 | Yes / no question (be verb) | 100.00% | 1.60 |
| 12 | Affirmative question | 96.67% | 2.23 |
| 13 | Wh-question | 90.00% | 2.17 |
| 14 | SV | 96.67% | 2.27 |
| 15 | SVC (V=be verb) (C=noun) | 96.67% | 1.60 |
| 16 | SVC (V=be verb) (C=pronoun) | 73.33% | 2.37 |
| 17 | SVC (V=be verb) (C=adjective) | 100.00% | 2.03 |
| 18 | SVC (V=general verb) (C=noun) | 100.00% | 2.03 |
| 19 | SVC (V=general verb) (C=adjective) | 100.00% | 2.77 |
| 20 | SVO (O=noun) | 93.33% | 1.77 |

| No. | Target grammatical items | Accuracy rates | Perceived difficulty levels |
|---|---|---|---|
| 21 | SVO (O=pronoun) | 100.00% | 1.77 |
| 22 | SVO (O=gerund) | 100.00% | 2.03 |
| 23 | SVO (O=to-infinitive) | 100.00% | 2.07 |
| 24 | SVO (O=how to-infinitive) | 100.00% | 2.43 |
| 25 | SVO (O=that-clause) | 100.00% | 1.97 |
| 26 | SVO (O=what-clause) | 96.67% | 2.73 |
| 27 | S+V+indirect object+direct object (noun) | 96.67% | 2.33 |
| 28 | S+V+indirect object+direct object (pronoun) | 93.33% | 2.47 |
| 29 | S + V + indirect object + direct object (how to-infinitive) | 93.33% | 2.40 |
| 30 | SVOC (C=noun) | 96.67% | 2.00 |
| 31 | SVOC (C=adjective) | 46.67% | 2.27 |
| 32 | There+be-verb ~ | 100.00% | 2.27 |
| 33 | It+be-verb+(for ~)+to-infinitive | 93.33% | 2.30 |
| 34 | S+tell, want+O+to-infinitive | 76.67% | 2.53 |
| 35 | Personal pronoun (subjective, possessive, objective) | 70.00% | 3.23 |
| 36 | Personal, demonstrative pronoun | 96.67% | 2.77 |
| 37 | Pronoun ('some') | 60.00% | 3.07 |
| 38 | Relative pronoun ('that' as subject) (restrictive use) | 53.33% | 3.77 |
| 39 | Relative pronoun ('which' as object) (restrictive use) | 70.00% | 3.40 |
| 40 | Present tense (be verb) | 73.33% | 3.73 |
| 41 | Present tense (general verb) | 73.33% | 3.37 |
| 42 | Past tense (be verb) | 56.67% | 3.30 |
| 43 | Past tense (general verb) | 90.00% | 2.37 |
| 44 | Past tense (irregular verb) | 56.67% | 3.50 |
| 45 | Present progressive | 70.00% | 3.17 |
| 46 | Past progressive | 56.67% | 2.90 |
| 47 | Present perfect (duration) | 73.33% | 3.00 |
| 48 | Present perfect (experience) | 60.00% | 3.00 |
| 49 | Present perfect (completion) | 76.67% | 3.37 |
| 50 | Auxiliary verb (will) (future) | 93.33% | 2.60 |
| 51 | Comparative (adjective ) (as ~ as) (as tall as) | 73.33% | 3.37 |
| 52 | Comparative (adjective) (-er) | 96.67% | 2.40 |

| No. | Target grammatical items | Accuracy rates | Perceived difficulty levels |
|---|---|---|---|
| 53 | Superlative (adjective) (-est) | 80.00% | 2.87 |
| 54 | Comparative (adjective) (as ~ as) (as beautiful as) | 73.33% | 3.50 |
| 55 | Comparative (adjective) (more + adjective) | 90.00% | 2.76 |
| 56 | Superlative (adjective) (most-adjective) | 83.33% | 2.70 |
| 57 | Comparative (adjective) (irregular) (as good as) | 63.34% | 3.73 |
| 58 | Comparative (adjective) (irregular) | 83.33% | 2.90 |
| 59 | Superlative (adjective) (irregular) | 73.33% | 3.10 |
| 60 | Comparative (adverb) (as ~ as) (as fast as) | 80.00% | 3.07 |
| 61 | Comparative (adverb) (-er) | 86.67% | 3.10 |
| 62 | Superlative (adverb) (-est) | 63.33% | 3.43 |
| 63 | Comparative (adverb) (as ~ as) (as slowly as) | 60.00% | 3.87 |
| 64 | Comparative (adverb) (more + adverb) | 56.67% | 3.67 |
| 65 | Superlative (most + adverb) | 46.67% | 4.03 |
| 66 | Comparative (adverb ) (as ~ as) (as well as) | 53.33% | 3.07 |
| 67 | Comparative (adverb) (irregular) | 60.00% | 3.40 |
| 68 | Superlative (adverb) (irregular) | 56.67% | 4.27 |
| 69 | To-infinitive (as noun) | 86.67% | 2.93 |
| 70 | To-infinitive (as adjective) | 50.00% | 3.57 |
| 71 | To-infinitive (as adverb) | 73.33% | 3.53 |
| 72 | Gerund (as object) | 93.33% | 2.43 |
| 73 | Present participle (as adjective) (pre-modification) | 86.67% | 2.83 |
| 74 | Past participle (as adjective) (post-modification) | 73.33% | 3.67 |
| 75 | Passive voice (present) | 70.00% | 3.67 |
| 76 | Passive voice (past) | 43.33% | 2.87 |
| 77 | SVC (V=general verb) (C=present participle) | 100.00% | 1.97 |
| 78 | SVC (V=general verb) (C=past participle) | 76.67% | 3.20 |
| 79 | SVO (O=if-clause) | 73.33% | 3.00 |
| 80 | S + V + indirect object + direct object (that-clause) | 93.33% | 2.07 |
| 81 | S + V + indirect object + direct object (what-clause) | 93.33% | 2.30 |
| 82 | S + V + indirect object + direct object (how-clause) | 83.33% | 2.73 |
| 83 | S+V+indirect object+direct object (if-clause) | 93.33% | 2.63 |
| 84 | SVOC (C=participle) | 96.67% | 2.50 |

| No. | Target grammatical items | Accuracy rates | Perceived difficulty levels |
|---|---|---|---|
| 85 | SVOC (V=causative verb) (C=bare infinitive) | 86.67% | 2.53 |
| 86 | SVOC (V=sensory verb) (C=bare infinitive) | 96.67% | 2.60 |
| 87 | S+seem+to-infinitive | 100.00% | 2.23 |
| 88 | It+seems+that-clause | 63.33% | 2.73 |
| 89 | Bare infinitive | 20.00% | 4.00 |
| 90 | Relative pronoun ('what') | 16.67% | 4.47 |
| 91 | Relative pronoun ('who' as nonrestrictive use) | 13.33% | 4.13 |
| 92 | Relative adverb ('where') | 40.00% | 3.80 |
| 93 | Relative adverb ('when') | 70.00% | 4.10 |
| 94 | Relative adverb ('why') | 50.00% | 4.62 |
| 95 | Relative adverb ('how') | 70.00% | 3.90 |
| 96 | Relative adverb ('where' as nonrestrictive use) | 20.00% | 4.57 |
| 97 | Relative adverb ('when' as nonrestrictive use) | 3.33% | 4.50 |
| 98 | Auxiliary verb (past) | 40.00% | 3.67 |
| 99 | Passive voice and modal auxiliary verb | 13.33% | 4.10 |
| 100 | Modal auxiliary verb and perfective aspect | 16.67% | 4.00 |
| 101 | Formal subject (that-clause) | 23.33% | 3.67 |
| 102 | Formal object (to-infinitive) | 43.33% | 3.67 |
| 103 | Formal object (that-clause) | 50.00% | 4.21 |
| 104 | Prsent perfect progressive | 53.33% | 3.90 |
| 105 | Past perfect | 50.00% | 3.47 |
| 106 | Subjunctive mood (past) | 30.00% | 3.80 |
| 107 | Subjunctive mood (past) (I wish ~) | 46.67% | 3.57 |
| 108 | Subjunctive mood (past perfect) | 13.33% | 4.07 |
| 109 | Participial construction (action continuing) | 53.33% | 3.73 |
| 110 | Participial construction (reason) | 26.67% | 4.27 |

## 4.2 Group 3

Group 3 consisted of grammatical items that the students regarded as easy to answer but answered incorrectly. In other words, this group of items reflects a gap between the students' actual performance and their perception; therefore, special

**Table 2.2**  *Grammatical Items in Group 3*

| No. | Target grammatical items | Accuracy rates | Perceived difficulty levels |
|---|---|---|---|
| 6 | Imperative (affirmative) (general verb) | 70.00% | 2.67 |
| 16 | SVC (V=be verb) (C=pronoun) | 73.33% | 2.37 |
| 31 | SVOC (C=adjective) | 46.67% | 2.27 |
| 34 | S+tell, want+O+to-infinitive | 76.67% | 2.53 |
| 46 | Past progressive | 56.67% | 2.90 |
| 47 | Present perfect (duration) | 73.33% | 3.00 |
| 48 | Present perfect (experience) | 60.00% | 3.00 |
| 76 | Passive voice (past) | 43.33% | 2.87 |
| 79 | SVO (O=if-clause) | 73.33% | 3.00 |
| 88 | It+seems+that-clause | 63.33% | 2.73 |

attention needs to be paid to these items by both the students and teachers. Table 2.2 presents the grammatical items that fell into Group 3. Eight of the total of ten items were those taught during junior high school. This suggests that some of the grammatical items that are considered basic for Japanese EFL university students are still unacquired.

## 4.2.1 Error analysis for Group 3

In this section, error analysis was conducted for three items whose accuracy rates were particularly low, that is, below 60%, among all items in Group 3. First, the target grammatical item for Number (hereafter No.) 31 was the SVOC sentence pattern, where C corresponds to an adjective[1]. The answer for this question was "You (S) should keep (V) this room (O) clean (C)," whose Japanese equivalent was "あなたはこの部屋をきれいにしておくべきです。"[2] The students tended to write such erroneous sentences as "*You (S) should keep (V) clean (C) this room (O),*" whose sentence pattern was SVCO, instead of SVOC. Although this pattern is taught at the junior high school level, the university students seemed to have difficulty with it. Tsuzuki (2003) argued that sentences with this pattern seldom appeared in junior high school English textbooks in Japan. This might have been one of the reasons why this pattern, though seemingly simple, was still problematic for the university students in this study.

The target item in No. 46 was the past progressive. The correct answer for this question was "I was reading a book then," which expressed the meaning of the Japanese sentence "私はその時本を読んでいました." Typical examples of errors were "I read the book then," using the past tense, and "I have read the book then," using the present perfect. These errors showed that the students failed to differentiate between various tenses: the past progressive, past, and present perfect.

No. 76 dealt with the passive voice. The correct answer for this question was "This machine was made in France," which corresponded to the Japanese sentence "この機械はフランスで作られました." An example of an incorrect answer for this question was "this machine ($\varphi$) made in France," where a be-verb ("was") is missing. This suggests that the students failed to combine a be-verb and a past participle to construct a sentence structure using the passive voice. It should be emphasized that all the grammatical structures discussed in this section are indeed taught in junior high school EFL classrooms and, therefore, can be considered simple enough for EFL beginners in terms of language complexity. The finding that the students in this study still had trouble with these structures suggests that not all the structures learned in junior high school are retained at the university level.

## 4.3 Group 4

The grammatical items in this group were those which the students failed to provide correct answers and which they perceived to be difficult to answer. Table 2.3 lists the items in Group 4. In contrast to the items in Group 3, nine out of the 11 items were those taught in high school, that is, those considered more advanced.

**Table 2.3**  *Grammatical Items in Group 4*

| No. | Target grammatical items | Accuracy rates | Perceived difficulty levels |
|---|---|---|---|
| 65 | Superlative (most + adverb) | 46.67% | 4.03 |
| 68 | Superlative (adverb) (irregular) | 56.67% | 4.27 |
| 89 | Bare infinitive | 20.00% | 4.00 |
| 90 | Relative pronoun ('what') | 16.67% | 4.47 |
| 91 | Relative pronoun ('who' as nonrestrictive use) | 13.33% | 4.13 |
| 96 | Relative adverb ('where' as nonrestrictive use) | 20.00% | 4.57 |
| 97 | Relative adverb ('when' as nonrestrictive use) | 3.33% | 4.50 |
| 99 | Passive voice and modal auxiliary verb | 13.33% | 4.10 |
| 100 | Modal auxiliary verb and perfective aspect | 16.67% | 4.00 |
| 108 | Subjunctive mood (past perfect) | 13.33% | 4.07 |
| 110 | Participial construction (reason) | 26.67% | 4.27 |

### 4.3.1 Error analysis for Group 4

Errors analysis was conducted for four items whose accuracy rates were extremely low, that is, below 15%. No. 91 asked about the nonrestrictive use of a relative pronoun "who." The original Japanese expression was "彼らには娘がいました.その娘は音楽を勉強するためにヨーロッパに行きました." The correct answer was "They had a daughter, who went to Europe to study music." Examples of errors were "They had a daughter, (φ) she goes to Eulope (*sic*) to study music" and "They had a daughter (φ) who she went to study music." In the former example, a relative pronoun was not used; in the latter, a relative pronoun was used, but "she" was inserted incorrectly, and a comma was missing. These examples demonstrate that the students lacked a fundamental understanding of how to use relative pronouns, their nonrestrictive use in particular, as a means of postmodification.

No. 97 was concerned with the nonrestrictive use of a relative adverb "when." The correct answer for this question was "Let's go to Hokkaido in June, when the weather is beautiful," whose meaning in Japanese was "*6月に北海道に行きましょう．その時は天気がいいですよ．*" A typical example of an incorrect answer was "Let's go to Hokkaido in June (φ) when it is sunny." Although the nonrestrictive use of relatives requires the use of a comma after the antecedent, a comma was missing in this answer. Similar to No. 91, when answering No. 97, the students seemed to fail to differentiate between the nonrestrictive and restrictive use of relative adverbs. Hashimoto (2016) also argued that the nonrestrictive use of relatives was one of the most difficult items for Japanese EFL students. Unlike Japanese, which uses premodification, English uses postmodification, where relatives are placed when nouns or noun phrases are postmodified. Japanese neither uses postmodification nor does it use the restrictive or nonrestrictive use of relatives; these differences between the two languages might have acted as interference and resulted in the students' errors.

In No. 99, the target was the passive voice coupled with a modal auxiliary verb. The Japanese sentence read, "*天気がいいと，富士山は新宿から見られます，*" and the correct answer was "In clear weather, Mt. Fuji can be seen from Shinjuku." An example of an incorrect answer was "In clear weather, Mt. Fuji can (φ) see from Shinjuku." In this erroneous sentence, an auxiliary verb "can" was appropriately used; however, the "be" verb was missing, and the past participle was not added. As this example shows, it seemed that the students were confused when they had to perform two operations simultaneously to realize their intended meaning.

No. 108 asked about the subjunctive past perfect. The Japanese sentence was "*もし十分なお金をもっていたら，もっと良いコンピューターを買っただろうに，*" and the corresponding English answer was "If I had had enough money, I would have bought a better computer." An example of an error was "If I had enough money, I would buy a better computer." Though the construction of the sentence in this example was correct, the subjunctive past was mistakenly used instead of the subjunctive past perfect, which was what should have been used. Another example of an error was "If I had enough money, I would have bought a better computer." In this case, the conditional clause (the if-clause...) was incorrectly written because the past tense was used, although the main clause was correctly constructed. The subjunctive is a difficult form to construct, because it is necessary to choose correct verb forms both in the if-clause and the main clause. Furthermore, the subjunctive past perfect is all the more difficult than the subjunctive past, because in constructing the former form, we need to use the past perfect by combining "had" and the past participle in the if-clause, while choosing an appropriate auxiliary (e.g., would, could, and might) and adding "have" and the past participle. Similar to No. 99, No. 108 requires multiple grammatical operations to derive the correct answer, and this might have confused the students in answering this question.

## 5. The relationship between Group 3 and Group 4

In this section, we will speculate on the relationship between Group 3 and Group 4 by focusing on two grammatical structures. The first structure was postmodification, which was used in No. 16 in Group 3 and No. 91 in Group 4. The target item for No. 16 contained a SVC sentence pattern. The correct answer for this question was "The pen on the desk is mine," where a prepositional phrase "on the desk" postmodifies "the pen." The Japanese prompt was "机の上のペンは私のです," where "机の上の" (on the desk) premodifies "ペン" (pen). The students assessed this item as easy, but the accuracy rate did not reach 80% (see Table 2.2). As was discussed in Section 4.3, No. 91 dealt with postmodification via a relative clause. The expected correct answer was "They had a daughter, who went to Europe to study music." In this sentence, a relative clause "who went to Europe to study music" postmodifiers a noun "daughter." The item in No. 16 is taught in junior high school, whereas the one in No. 91 is taught in high school; therefore, the former is considered a more basic, simpler form of postmodification, and the latter to be a more advanced, complicated form. When the answers to these two questions were analyzed, it was found that if the students could not provide a correct answer to No. 16, they could not give a correct answer to No. 91, either. That is, we could speculate that if the students could not postmodify a noun with a prepositional phrase, they could not postmodify a noun with a relative clause, either.

The second structure examined was the passive voice. No. 76 targeted the passive voice in a simple form which is taught in junior high school: "This machine was made in France." On the other hand, in No. 99, the answer was "In clear weather, Mt. Fuji can be seen from Shinjuku." The grammatical item in No. 99 is more complicated because the passive voice is combined with an auxiliary verb; this structure is taught in high school. Here 82% of the students who failed to give correct answers in No. 76 also failed to do so in No. 99. Therefore, it can be said that if the students could not construct a sentence in the passive voice, they likely could not make a sentence by combining the passive voice and an auxiliary verb, either. These two examples suggest an acquisition order in which there are early-acquired items (i.e., postmodification by a prepositional phrase and the simple passive voice) and late-acquired items (*i.e.*, postmodification by a relative clause and the passive voice combined with an auxiliary verb).

## 6. Conclusion

The present study attempted to clarify the grammatical items that are especially problematic for Japanese students at the low-intermediate EFL level by analyzing the accuracy rates and difficulty levels of a grammar test. The analysis revealed the following findings:

1) The grammatical items that the students tended to regard as easy to answer but answered incorrectly were mostly those taught during junior high school, including the SVOC sentence pattern, the past progressive, and the

passive voice.
2) The items that they tended to consider difficult to answer and answered incorrectly were mostly those taught during high school, such as the nonrestrictive use of relative pronouns and adverbs, the passive voice combined with an auxiliary verb, and the subjunctive past perfect.
3) For some grammatical structures, the students could not produce advanced forms without being able to produce their basic counterparts in the same categories, such as postmodification and the passive voice.

These findings offer several pedagogical implications. First, teachers need to pay special attention to the fact that their students still have difficulty with some grammatical items that they regard as easy. The majority of these items is taught in junior high school, and thus are basic structures. However, in this study, the students failed to reach the sufficient acquisition level of 80% for these items. As the third finding implies, the students cannot acquire an advanced structure without acquiring its simple counterpart in the same category, such as postmodification. It is thus necessary to provide students with careful grammar instruction that aims to help them acquire basic grammatical items taught in EFL classrooms in junior high school.

Moreover, teachers need to give their students targeted instruction for those grammatical structures that are perceived as difficult and are prone to errors (i.e., mostly complicated advanced grammatical structures dealt with in high school EFL classrooms). Some of these grammatical items, such as relative pronouns and adverbs, reflect differences between Japanese and English, with the possibility of inducing interference for EFL students. Teachers need to thus carefully explain where the differences between the two languages lie and give them enough input to overcome possible interference.

Finally, to foster the students' grammatical competence, it is important to give them ample opportunities to transform input into intake, thereby transforming their declarative knowledge into procedural knowledge; this is especially the case for items that are problematic for students. Input containing these items needs to occur through reading and listening and be followed by written/oral production and output in meaningful communicative contexts.

The present study had several limitations. First, there was a limited number of participants at the low-intermediate EFL level. Next, the accuracy rate and difficulty levels for each grammatical item were examined for only one question on the grammar test. Further studies are thus needed to uncover a clearer picture of Japanese EFL students' grammatical competence, through a more detailed investigation of the accuracy rates and difficulty levels of various grammatical items.

## Notes

1. The grammar test for the university students consists of two parts, each of which uses serial question numbers starting from 1. Also, the same question is assigned different question numbers on the tests for the university students and high school students. Therefore, in order to avoid confusion, throughout the three studies, the reference number, rather than the question numbers, are used whenever the results of the analysis are discussed by referring to the target grammatical items.
2. The parts which the students are required to answer in the questions are underlined by straight lines, while the errors that they made in the sentences are marked by wavy lines. This notation system is used in all of the studies (Studies 1, 2 and 3).

# Chapter 3

*Study 2*

# EFL students' and teachers' perceived difficulty levels and accuracy rates for different grammatical items

## 1. Introduction

Study 1 focused on the EFL students' perceived difficulty levels of different grammatical items. The findings of this study clarifies which items are difficult for the students and therefore require more time for learning. However, the students' perspection only is not enough. For effective grammar teaching and learning, teachers' perspective is also important.

Studies that attempted to examine students' and teachers' perceived difficulty levels of different grammatical items are scarce, and one example of those studies is a survey conducted by Hidai et al. (2012), who examined Japanese EFL students' levels of "understanding," rather than their levels of "difficulty," of various grammatical items. That is, Hidai et al. investigated how the students perceived their understanding of 66 grammatical items chosen from those taught in junior high school and high school. It was found that the students answered that they understood most of these items at the sufficient level. When their perceived "understanding" levels were compared with those of teachers, it was found that the students' levels were considerably higher than the teachers' levels, which suggests that the students overestimated their level of grammatical competence. The greatest gap between the students' and teachers' perceptions was clearly observed in the complex sentence structure. The grammatical items covered in Hidai et al.'s study, however, were not comprehensive enough, in that the study did not examine all the items that were expected to be taught at the Japanese secondary school level. In addition, no study has attempted to explore the relationships of (1) students' and (2) teachers' perceived difficulty levels for different grammatical items, and (3) the students' accuracy scores on those items. Study 2, therefore, was conducted, assuming that without accurate information on these points, any effective EFL grammar teaching for Japanese students could not be developed.

## 2. Purpose of the study

The ultimate goal of the present study was to provide baseline information that can be utilized to develop effective EFL teaching for Japanese EFL students at the low-intermediate level — the students who need basic grammatical knowledge that Otsu (2012) regarded as essential for communication in EFL. For this purpose, the study attempted to examine Japanese university students' perceived difficulty levels for various grammatical items, Japanese EFL teachers' perceived difficulty levels of those items, and finally, the relationships between students' accuracy rates and the difficulty levels of the two groups. Specifically, the following four research questions were posed.

1) Which grammatical items do students perceive as difficult/easy to answer?
2) Which grammatical items do teachers perceive their students as having much/little difficulty with?
3) Are there any gaps between the students' and teachers' perceptions?
4) How do the students' accuracy rates relate to the students' and teachers' perceptions?

# 3. Procedure

## 3.1 Participants

The present study involved two groups of participants. The first group consisted of 40 Japanese university EFL students, who had also participated in Study 1. They were first-year students majoring in English at a four-year Japanese university. Their English proficiency level was considered at the low-intermediate level, with the average TOEIC® (Listening and Reading) score of 320. 67 points. The other group comprised 53 Japanese EFL teachers; 13 of them were university English teachers, whereas the remaining 40 were Japanese EFL high school teachers. The study aimed to provide useful information for teachers at both the high school and university levels; therefore, a composite group of teachers was asked to participate in the study.

## 3.2 Data collection

### 3.2.1 Grammar test for the students

For the sake of clarity, the grammar test and questionnaire given to the participants will be explained again.

Following Hashimoto and Kamimura (2015) and Hashimoto (2016), a grammar test was prepared. The test consisted of 110 questions, each of which was targeted at a different grammatical item. The test was comprehensive enough to cover all the grammatical items listed in *the Course of Study for Junior High Schools, Foreign Languages* (MEXT, 2008) and *the Course of Study for High Schools, Foreign Languages, English* (MEXT, 2010).

The test was made up of two parts, each of which contained 55 questions. The students took the first part in 35 minutes, and a week later they took the second part, again in 35 minutes. Whenever they answered each question, they scored the difficulty level of answering the question on a six-point Likert scale, where one signified "very easy" and six, "very difficult."

Figure 3.1 shows an example of a question on the test. As was mentioned before, the present study aimed to provide useful information needed to develop grammar teaching for EFL students at the low-intermediate level. Therefore, in the study the students took the test in early April, when the Japanese academic year started, so that their scores on the test could be considered to reflect the grammatical competence and perceived difficulty levels for Japanese high school EFL students soon after graduating from high school and, simultaneously, university EFL students soon after entering university.

---

健は由美よりも背が高いです。　　　　very easy ⟷ very difficult
Ken (　　　　　　　　　　　) Yumi.　 1　2　3　4　5　6

Expected answer: Ken (is taller than) Yumi.

---

***Figure 3.1*** An example of questions used in the grammar test.

### 3.2.2 Questionnaire for the teachers

A questionnaire for the teachers was prepared based on the grammar test given to the students. They were asked to assess the level of difficulty that their students would have when answering each question on the test. Figure 3.2 displays an example of questions used in the questionnaire. Both the expected answer and target grammatical item for each question were shown on the questionnaire for the teachers.

---

健は由美よりも背が高いです。　　　　very easy ⟷ very difficult
Ken (　　　　　　　　　　　) Yumi.　 1　2　3　4　5　6

Expected answer: Ken (is taller than) Yumi.
Target grammatical item: Comparative (adjective) (-er)

---

***Figure 3.2*** An example of questions used in the survey.

# 4. Analysis

## 4.1 Accuracy rates

The average accuracy rate for each question was calculated. Referring to Brown (1973) and Krashen (1977), 80% accuracy was determined as the threshold level to judge whether or not a given target grammatical item was acquired. A total of 110 grammatical items were thus classified into two groups: (1) the grammatical items with the accuracy rates equal to or above 80%, and (2) those with the accuracy rates below 80%.

## 4.2 Students' perceived difficulty levels

The students' average perceived difficulty level was examined for each item. The items were also categorized into two groups: (1) the items for which the students' average perceived difficulty levels were equal to or above 3.50, the median on the assessment scale, and (2) those below 3.50.

## 4.3 Teachers' difficulty assessment

The teachers' average difficulty assessment for each item was also calculated. The items were then categorized into two groups: (1) the items for which the teachers' average perceived difficulty levels were equal to or above 3.50 and (2) those below 3.50.

## 4.4 Comparison of the students' and teachers' perceived difficulty levels

The students' and teachers' average perceived difficulty levels were compared for each item. Analysis was conducted to detect in which grammatical items similarities and differences between the two could be observed. Further analysis was attempted to examine whether or not the students' and teachers' perceptions were related to the accuracy rates for the various grammatical items.

# 5. Results and discussion

## 5.1 Average accuracy rates and perceived difficulty levels

Table 3.1 shows the average accuracy rate and the perceived difficulty levels of the students and teachers for each grammatical item.

In the following sections, the accuracy rates and perceived difficulty levels of the students and teachers will be compared to explore both similarities and differences between the two.

**Table 3.1** *Average Accuracy Rates and Perceived Difficulty Levels of the Students and Teachers for Each Grammatical Item*

| No. | Target grammatical items | Accuracy rates | Students' perceived difficulty levels | Teachers' perceived difficulty levels | Differences (Teachers-Students) |
|---|---|---|---|---|---|
| 1 | Simple sentence | 96.67% | 1.87 | 1.96 | 0.09 |
| 2 | Compound sentence | 93.33% | 2.57 | 2.94 | 0.37 |
| 3 | Complex sentence | 100.00% | 2.30 | 3.02 | 0.72 |
| 4 | Positive declarative sentence | 100.00% | 1.57 | 1.22 | −0.35 |
| 5 | Negative declarative sentence | 100.00% | 2.00 | 1.43 | −0.57 |
| 6 | Imperative (affirmative) (general verb) | 70.00% | 2.67 | 1.65 | −1.02 |
| 7 | Positive imperative sentence (be verb) | 100.00% | 2.53 | 1.94 | −0.59 |
| 8 | Negative imperative sentence (general verb) | 100.00% | 1.83 | 1.41 | −0.42 |
| 9 | Negative imperative sentence (be verb) | 100.00% | 2.40 | 1.94 | −0.46 |
| 10 | Yes / no question (general verb) | 100.00% | 2.10 | 1.87 | −0.23 |
| 11 | Yes / no question (be verb) | 100.00% | 1.60 | 1.28 | −0.32 |
| 12 | Affirmative question | 96.67% | 2.23 | 2.40 | 0.17 |
| 13 | Wh-question | 90.00% | 2.17 | 2.89 | 0.72 |
| 14 | SV | 96.67% | 2.27 | 3.24 | 0.97 |
| 15 | SVC (V=be verb) (C=noun) | 96.67% | 1.60 | 1.15 | −0.45 |
| 16 | SVC (V=be verb) (C=pronoun) | 73.33% | 2.37 | 3.00 | 0.63 |

| No. | Target grammatical items | Accuracy rates | Students' perceived difficulty levels | Teachers' perceived difficulty levels | Differences (Teachers-Students) |
|---|---|---|---|---|---|
| 17 | SVC (V=be verb) (C=adjective) | 100.00% | 2.03 | 1.69 | −0.34 |
| 18 | SVC (V=general verb) (C=noun) | 100.00% | 2.03 | 1.67 | −0.36 |
| 19 | SVC (V=general verb) (C=adjective) | 100.00% | 2.77 | 3.49 | 0.72 |
| 20 | SVO (O=noun) | 93.33% | 1.77 | 1.78 | 0.01 |
| 21 | SVO (O=pronoun) | 100.00% | 1.77 | 1.43 | −0.34 |
| 22 | SVO (O=gerund) | 100.00% | 2.03 | 2.52 | 0.49 |
| 23 | SVO (O=to-infinitive) | 100.00% | 2.07 | 2.72 | 0.65 |
| 24 | SVO (O=how to-infinitive) | 100.00% | 2.43 | 3.37 | 0.94 |
| 25 | SVO (O=that-clause) | 100.00% | 1.97 | 3.54 | 1.57 |
| 26 | SVO (O=what-clause) | 96.67% | 2.73 | 4.00 | 1.27 |
| 27 | S+V+indirect object+direct object (noun) | 96.67% | 2.33 | 3.22 | 0.89 |
| 28 | S+V+indirect object+direct object (pronoun) | 93.33% | 2.47 | 3.02 | 0.55 |
| 29 | S + V + indirect object + direct object (how to-infinitive) | 93.33% | 2.40 | 3.47 | 1.07 |
| 30 | SVOC (C=noun) | 96.67% | 2.00 | 2.82 | 0.82 |
| 31 | SVOC (C=adjective) | 46.67% | 2.27 | 3.93 | 1.66 |
| 32 | There+be-verb ~ | 100.00% | 2.27 | 2.84 | 0.57 |
| 33 | It+be-verb+(for ~)+to-infinitive | 93.33% | 2.30 | 3.63 | 1.33 |
| 34 | S+tell, want+O+to-infinitive | 76.67% | 2.53 | 3.80 | 1.27 |
| 35 | Personal pronoun (subjective, possessive, objective) | 70.00% | 3.23 | 3.33 | 0.10 |
| 36 | Personal, demonstrative pronoun | 96.67% | 2.77 | 2.86 | 0.09 |
| 37 | Pronoun ('some') | 60.00% | 3.07 | 2.98 | −0.09 |
| 38 | Relative pronoun ('that' as subject) (restrictive use) | 53.33% | 3.77 | 4.39 | 0.62 |
| 39 | Relative pronoun ('which' as object) (restrictive use) | 70.00% | 3.40 | 4.24 | 0.84 |
| 40 | Present tense (be verb) | 73.33% | 3.73 | 2.44 | −1.29 |
| 41 | Present tense (general verb) | 73.33% | 3.37 | 2.80 | −0.57 |
| 42 | Past tense (be verb) | 56.67% | 3.30 | 1.98 | −1.32 |
| 43 | Past tense (general verb) | 90.00% | 2.37 | 1.96 | −0.41 |
| 44 | Past tense (irregular verb) | 56.67% | 3.50 | 2.46 | −1.04 |
| 45 | Present progressive | 70.00% | 3.17 | 2.06 | −1.11 |
| 46 | Past progressive | 56.67% | 2.90 | 2.24 | −0.66 |
| 47 | Present perfect (duration) | 73.33% | 3.00 | 3.55 | 0.55 |
| 48 | Present perfect (experience) | 60.00% | 3.00 | 3.57 | 0.57 |
| 49 | Present perfect (completion) | 76.67% | 3.37 | 3.48 | 0.11 |

| No. | Target grammatical items | Accuracy rates | Students' perceived difficulty levels | Teachers' perceived difficulty levels | Differ-ences (Teachers-Students) |
|---|---|---|---|---|---|
| 50 | Auxiliary verb (will) (future) | 93.33% | 2.60 | 2.61 | 0.01 |
| 51 | Comparative (adjective ) (as ~ as) (as tall as) | 73.33% | 3.37 | 2.91 | −0.46 |
| 52 | Comparative (adjective) (-er) | 96.67% | 2.40 | 2.26 | −0.14 |
| 53 | Superlative (adjective) (-est) | 80.00% | 2.87 | 2.43 | −0.44 |
| 54 | Comparative (adjective) (as ~ as) (as beautiful as) | 73.33% | 3.50 | 3.06 | −0.44 |
| 55 | Comparative (adjective) (more + adjective) | 90.00% | 2.76 | 2.94 | 0.18 |
| 56 | Superlative (adjective) (most + adjective) | 83.33% | 2.70 | 2.78 | 0.08 |
| 57 | Comparative (adjective) (irregular) (as good as) | 63.34% | 3.73 | 3.52 | −0.21 |
| 58 | Comparative (adjective) (irregular) | 83.33% | 2.90 | 2.87 | −0.03 |
| 59 | Superlative (adjective) (irregular) | 73.33% | 3.10 | 2.74 | −0.36 |
| 60 | Comparative (adverb) (as ~ as) (as fast as) | 80.00% | 3.07 | 3.56 | 0.49 |
| 61 | Comparative (adverb) (-er) | 86.67% | 3.10 | 2.87 | −0.23 |
| 62 | Superlative (adverb) (-est) | 63.33% | 3.43 | 3.15 | −0.28 |
| 63 | Comparative (adverb) (as ~ as) (as slowly as) | 60.00% | 3.87 | 3.65 | −0.22 |
| 64 | Comparative (adverb) (more + adverb) | 56.67% | 3.67 | 3.37 | −0.30 |
| 65 | Superlative (most + adverb) | 46.67% | 4.03 | 3.59 | −0.44 |
| 66 | Comparative (adverb) (as ~ as) (as well as) | 53.33% | 3.07 | 3.61 | 0.54 |
| 67 | Comparative (adverb) (irregular) | 60.00% | 3.40 | 3.06 | −0.34 |
| 68 | Superlative (adverb) (irregular) | 56.67% | 4.27 | 3.69 | −0.58 |
| 69 | To-infinitive (as noun) | 86.67% | 2.93 | 2.57 | −0.36 |
| 70 | To-infinitive (as adjective) | 50.00% | 3.57 | 3.67 | 0.10 |
| 71 | To-infinitive (as adverb) | 73.33% | 3.53 | 3.28 | −0.25 |
| 72 | Gerund (as object) | 93.33% | 2.43 | 2.80 | 0.37 |
| 73 | Present participle (as adjective) (pre-modification) | 86.67% | 2.83 | 2.83 | 0.00 |
| 74 | Past participle (as adjective) (post-modification) | 73.33% | 3.67 | 4.07 | 0.40 |
| 75 | Passive voice (present) | 70.00% | 3.67 | 3.39 | −0.28 |
| 76 | Passive voice (past) | 43.33% | 2.87 | 2.94 | 0.07 |
| 77 | SVC (V=general verb) (C=present participle) | 100.00% | 1.97 | 3.21 | 1.24 |
| 78 | SVC (V=general verb) (C=past participle) | 76.67% | 3.20 | 4.34 | 1.14 |
| 79 | SVO (O=if-clause) | 73.33% | 3.00 | 4.44 | 1.44 |
| 80 | S+V+indirect object+direct object (that-clause) | 93.33% | 2.07 | 4.15 | 2.08 |
| 81 | S+V+indirect object+direct object (what-clause) | 93.33% | 2.30 | 3.87 | 1.57 |
| 82 | S+V+indirect object+direct object (how-clause) | 83.33% | 2.73 | 3.92 | 1.19 |
| 83 | S+V+indirect object+direct object (if-clause) | 93.33% | 2.63 | 3.88 | 1.25 |

| No. | Target grammatical items | Accuracy rates | Students' perceived difficulty levels | Teachers' perceived difficulty levels | Differ-ences (Teachers-Students) |
|---|---|---|---|---|---|
| 84 | SVOC (C=participle) | 96.67% | 2.50 | 4.04 | 1.54 |
| 85 | SVOC (V=causative verb) (C=bare infinitive) | 86.67% | 2.53 | 4.07 | 1.54 |
| 86 | SVOC (V=sensory verb) (C=bare infinitive) | 96.67% | 2.60 | 4.14 | 1.54 |
| 87 | S+seem+to-infinitive | 100.00% | 2.23 | 3.80 | 1.57 |
| 88 | It+seems+that-clause | 63.33% | 2.73 | 3.94 | 1.21 |
| 89 | Bare infinitive | 20.00% | 4.00 | 4.59 | 0.59 |
| 90 | Relative pronoun ('what') | 16.67% | 4.47 | 4.85 | 0.38 |
| 91 | Relative pronoun ('who' as nonrestrictive use) | 13.33% | 4.13 | 5.11 | 0.98 |
| 92 | Relative adverb ('where') | 40.00% | 3.80 | 4.61 | 0.81 |
| 93 | Relative adverb ('when') | 70.00% | 4.10 | 4.65 | 0.55 |
| 94 | Relative adverb ('why') | 50.00% | 4.62 | 4.83 | 0.21 |
| 95 | Relative adverb ('how') | 70.00% | 3.90 | 4.56 | 0.66 |
| 96 | Relative adverb ('where' as nonrestrictive use) | 20.00% | 4.57 | 5.21 | 0.64 |
| 97 | Relative adverb ('when' as nonrestrictive use) | 3.33% | 4.50 | 5.33 | 0.83 |
| 98 | Auxiliary verb (past) | 40.00% | 3.67 | 3.26 | −0.41 |
| 99 | Passive voice and modal auxiliary verb | 13.33% | 4.10 | 4.52 | 0.42 |
| 100 | Modal auxiliary verb and perfective aspect | 16.67% | 4.00 | 5.26 | 1.26 |
| 101 | Formal subject (that-clause) | 23.33% | 3.67 | 4.28 | 0.61 |
| 102 | Formal object (to-infinitive) | 43.33% | 3.67 | 4.85 | 1.18 |
| 103 | Formal object (that-clause) | 50.00% | 4.21 | 5.02 | 0.81 |
| 104 | Prsent perfect progressive | 53.33% | 3.90 | 4.59 | 0.69 |
| 105 | Past perfect | 50.00% | 3.47 | 4.80 | 1.33 |
| 106 | Subjunctive mood (past) | 30.00% | 3.80 | 5.06 | 1.26 |
| 107 | Subjunctive mood (past) (I wish ~) | 46.67% | 3.57 | 4.69 | 1.12 |
| 108 | Subjunctive mood (past perfect) | 13.33% | 4.07 | 5.44 | 1.37 |
| 109 | Participial construction (action continuing) | 53.33% | 3.73 | 4.85 | 1.12 |
| 110 | Participial construction (reason) | 26.67% | 4.27 | 5.13 | 0.86 |
| SD | | 25.74% | 0.77 | 1.06 | 0.29 |
| Average | | 72.79% | 2.98 | 3.35 | 0.37 |

## 5.2 Comparison between the students' and teachers' perceived difficulty levels

### 5.2.1 Similarities

Correlation analysis revealed that the student and teacher groups were significantly correlated in terms of their perceived difficulty levels ($r=.708$, $p<.01$). Next, the top ten items on the students' and teachers' lists of difficulty levels were compared; similarly, the bottom ten items on the two groups' difficulty lists were compared. As can be seen in Tables 3.2 and 3.3, out of the ten grammatical items, six items appeared on both lists: No. 90 (relative pronoun "what"), No. 91 (relative pronoun "who" as nonrestrictive use), No. 96 (relative adverb "where" as nonrestrictive use), No. 97 (relative adverb "when" as nonrestrictive use), No. 103 (formal object (that-clause)), and No. 110 (participial construction (reason)). All of these items are included in *The Course of Study for High Schools, Foreign Languages, English* (MEXT, 2010) and are thus advanced types of grammatical items.

**Table 3.2**  *Ten Grammatical Items that the Students Regarded as Relatively Difficult*

| No. | Target grammatical items | Students' perceived difficulty levels |
|---|---|---|
| 94 | Relative adverb ('why') | 4.62 |
| 96 | Relative adverb ('where' as nonrestrictive use) | 4.57 |
| 97 | Relative adverb ('when' as nonrestrictive use) | 4.50 |
| 90 | Relative pronoun ('what') | 4.47 |
| 68 | Superlative (adverb) (irregular) | 4.27 |
| 110 | Participial construction (reason) | 4.27 |
| 103 | Formal object (that-clause) | 4.21 |
| 91 | Relative pronoun ('who' as nonrestrictive use) | 4.13 |
| 93 | Relative adverb ('when') | 4.10 |
| 99 | Passive voice and modal auxiliary verb | 4.10 |

**Table 3.3** *Ten Grammatical Items that the Teachers Regarded as Relatively Difficult*

| No. | Target grammatical items | Teachers' perceived difficulty levels |
|---|---|---|
| 108 | Subjunctive mood (past perfect) | 5.44 |
| 97 | Relative adverb ('when' as nonrestrictive use) | 5.33 |
| 100 | Modal auxiliary verb and perfective aspect | 5.26 |
| 96 | Relative adverb ('where' as nonrestrictive use) | 5.21 |
| 110 | Participial construction (reason) | 5.13 |
| 91 | Relative pronoun ('who' as nonrestrictive use) | 5.11 |
| 106 | Subjunctive mood (past) | 5.06 |
| 103 | Formal object (that-clause) | 5.02 |
| 90 | Relative pronoun ('what') | 4.85 |
| 102 | Formal object (to-infinitive) | 4.85 |

It seems that relative clauses where relative pronouns and adverbs are used are particularly problematic from both the students' and teachers' points of view.

Tables 3.4 and 3.5 display the grammatical items that the students and teachers, respectively, considered relatively easy. Eleven items are shown in Table 3.4, because two items had the same score and ranked eleventh on the difficulty scale.

As Tables 3.4 and 3.5 demonstrate, the items regarded as easy by the students and teachers were mostly those listed on *The Course of Study for Junior High Schools, Foreign Languages* (MEXT, 2008). Again, six items appear on both lists: No. 4 (positive declarative sentence), No. 8 (negative imperative sentence (general verb)), No. 11 (yes/no question involving a be-verb), No. 15 (SVC where V is a be-verb and C is a noun), No. 20 (SVO where O is a noun), and No. 21 (SVO where O is a pronoun). These six items are all related to basic sentence structures to be learned at the beginning stage of EFL learning.

Further attempts were made to detect similarities between

**Table 3.4**  *Eleven Grammatical Items that the Students Regarded as Relatively Easy*

| No. | Target grammatical items | Students' perceived difficulty levels |
|---|---|---|
| 4 | Positive declarative sentence | 1.57 |
| 11 | Yes / no question (be verb) | 1.60 |
| 15 | SVC (V=be verb) (C=noun) | 1.60 |
| 20 | SVO (O=noun) | 1.77 |
| 21 | SVO (O=pronoun) | 1.77 |
| 8 | Negative imperative sentence (general verb) | 1.83 |
| 1 | Simple sentence | 1.87 |
| 25 | SVO (O=that-clause) | 1.97 |
| 77 | SVC (V=general verb) (C=present participle) | 1.97 |
| 5 | Negative declarative sentence | 2.00 |
| 30 | SVOC (C=noun) | 2.00 |

**Table 3.5**  *Ten Grammatical Items that the Teachers Regarded as Relatively Easy*

| No. | Target grammatical items | Teachers' perceived difficulty levels |
|---|---|---|
| 15 | SVC (V=be verb) (C=noun) | 1.15 |
| 4 | Positve declarative sentence | 1.22 |
| 11 | Yes / no question (be verb) | 1.28 |
| 8 | Negative imperative sentence (general verb) | 1.41 |
| 5 | Negative declarative sentence | 1.43 |
| 21 | SVO (O=pronoun) | 1.43 |
| 6 | Imperative (affirmative) (general verb) | 1.65 |
| 18 | SVC (V=general verb) (C=noun) | 1.67 |
| 17 | SVC (V=be verb) (C=adjective) | 1.69 |
| 20 | SVO (O=noun) | 1.78 |

**Table 3.6** *Ten Grammatical Items with Low Accuracy Rates*

| No. | Target grammatical items | Accuracy rates | Students' perceived difficulty levels | Teachers' perceived difficulty levels |
|---|---|---|---|---|
| 97 | Relative adverb ('when' as nonrestrictive use) | 3.33% | 4.50 | 5.33 |
| 91 | Relative pronoun ('who' as nonrestrictive use) | 13.33% | 4.13 | 5.11 |
| 99 | Passive voice and modal auxiliary verb | 13.33% | 4.10 | 4.52 |
| 108 | Subjunctive mood (past perfect) | 13.33% | 4.07 | 5.44 |
| 90 | Relative pronoun ('what') | 16.67% | 4.47 | 4.85 |
| 100 | Modal auxiliary verb and perfective aspect | 16.67% | 4.00 | 5.26 |
| 89 | Bare infinitive | 20.00% | 4.00 | 4.59 |
| 96 | Relative adverb ('where' as nonrestrictive use) | 20.00% | 4.57 | 5.21 |
| 101 | Formal subject (that-clause) | 23.33% | 3.67 | 4.28 |
| 110 | Participial construction (reason) | 26.67% | 4.27 | 5.13 |

the students' and teachers' perceived levels of difficulty while considering the accuracy rates for the grammatical items. First, ten grammatical items with low accuracy rates (i.e., below 30%) were focused upon. All of these items were listed in *The Course of Study for High Schools, Foreign Languages, English* (MEXT, 2010). As Table 3.6 illustrates, both the students and teachers considered these items difficult, with the average difficulty level above 3.50.

Next, the grammatical items with high accuracy rates were examined. Table 3.7 summarizes the result of the analysis.

For 19 items, 100% accuracy rates were observed. Seventeen of the items, which corresponded to basic sentence structures,

**Table 3.7** *Ten Grammatical Items with High Accuracy Rates*

| No. | Target grammatical items | Accuracy rates | Students' perceived difficulty levels | Teachers' perceived difficulty levels |
|---|---|---|---|---|
| 3 | Complex sentence | 100.00% | 2.30 | 3.02 |
| 4 | Positive declarative sentence | 100.00% | 1.57 | 1.22 |
| 5 | Negative declarative sentence | 100.00% | 2.00 | 1.43 |
| 7 | Positive imperative sentence (be verb) | 100.00% | 2.53 | 1.94 |
| 8 | Negative imperative sentence (general verb) | 100.00% | 1.83 | 1.41 |
| 9 | Negative imperative sentence (be verb) | 100.00% | 2.40 | 1.94 |
| 10 | Yes / no question (general verb) | 100.00% | 2.10 | 1.87 |
| 11 | Yes / no question (be verb) | 100.00% | 1.60 | 1.28 |
| 17 | SVC (V=be verb) (C=adjective) | 100.00% | 2.03 | 1.69 |
| 18 | SVC (V=general verb) (C=noun) | 100.00% | 2.03 | 1.67 |
| 19 | SVC (C=general verb) (C=adjective) | 100.00% | 2.77 | 3.49 |
| 21 | SVO (O=pronoun) | 100.00% | 1.77 | 1.43 |
| 22 | SVO (O=gerund) | 100.00% | 2.03 | 2.52 |
| 23 | SVO (O=to-infinitive) | 100.00% | 2.07 | 2.72 |
| 24 | SVO (O=how to-infinitive) | 100.00% | 2.43 | 3.37 |
| 25 | SVO (O=that-clause) | 100.00% | 1.97 | 3.54 |
| 32 | There+be-verb~ | 100.00% | 2.27 | 2.84 |
| 77 | SVC (V=general verb) (C=present participle) | 100.00% | 1.97 | 3.21 |
| 87 | S+seem+to-infinitive | 100.00% | 2.23 | 3.80 |

were found to be those taught in junior high school.  The students perceived all of these 19 items to be easy, with the score below 3.5 points.  The teachers also considered most of them easy, with the exception of No. 25, which asked about the SVO pattern where O is a "that" clause, and No. 87, which targeted the "S + seem + to-infinitive" sentence construction.

## 5.3 Differences

### 5.3.1 Grammatical items that the students perceived to be less difficult than did the teachers

Out of a total of 110 grammatical items, the students perceived 71 items to be easier than did the teachers.  Table 3.8 displays the items for which the students scored more than one point lower than the teachers on the difficulty assessment scale.  Twenty-five items were found to be of this type, and 19 of them were items taught in high school.  The greatest difference between the students' and teachers' difficulty levels was observed in the sentence construction "S + V + indirect object + direct object (that-clause)" (No. 80).

The students perceived only six of these 25 items to be relatively difficult, with scores above 3.50, whereas the teachers considered as many as 23 items highly difficult.  When the accuracy rates were considered, it was found that, although the students found them easier, they failed to demonstrate 80% accuracy for 12 out of the 25 items.

When closely examined by combining the accuracy rates and difficulty levels, those 25 items could be classified into four categories.  The classification scheme is shown in Table 3.9.

Group 1 consists of grammatical items for which high accuracy rates were observed, and which both the students and teachers regarded as relatively easy.  Forty-one items fell into this group.  Table 3.10 illustrates two representative examples in this group, with the high accuracy rates that exceeded 90%.  This result suggests that Japanese teachers do not have to pay too much attention to these items, which are related to basic English sentence patterns, in EFL classrooms, even though the students

**Table 3.8** *Grammatical Items that the Students Perceived to Be Much Easier than Did the Teachers*

| No. | Target grammatical items | Accuracy rates | Students' perceived difficulty levels | Teachers' perceived difficulty levels | Differences (Teachers-Students) | Groups |
|---|---|---|---|---|---|---|
| 80 | S+V+indirect object+direct object (that-clause) | 93.33% | 2.07 | 4.15 | 2.08 | 2 |
| 31 | SVOC (C=adjective) | 46.67% | 2.27 | 3.93 | 1.66 | 3 |
| 81 | S+V+indirect object+direct object (what-clause) | 93.33% | 2.30 | 3.87 | 1.57 | 2 |
| 25 | SVO (O=that-clause) | 100.00% | 1.97 | 3.54 | 1.57 | 2 |
| 87 | S+seem+to-infinitive | 100.00% | 2.23 | 3.8 | 1.57 | 2 |
| 85 | SVOC (V=causative verb) (C=bare infinitive) | 86.67% | 2.53 | 4.07 | 1.54 | 2 |
| 84 | SVOC (C=participle) | 96.67% | 2.50 | 4.04 | 1.54 | 2 |
| 86 | SVOC (V=sensory verb) (C=bare infinitive) | 96.67% | 2.60 | 4.14 | 1.54 | 2 |
| 79 | SVO (O=if-clause) | 73.33% | 3.00 | 4.44 | 1.44 | 3 |
| 108 | Subjunctive mood (past perfect) | 13.33% | 4.07 | 5.44 | 1.37 | 4 |
| 33 | It+be-verb+(for ~)+to-infinitive | 93.33% | 2.30 | 3.63 | 1.33 | 3 |
| 105 | Past perfect | 50.00% | 3.47 | 4.8 | 1.33 | 2 |
| 26 | SVO (O=what-clause) | 96.67% | 2.73 | 4.00 | 1.27 | 2 |
| 34 | S+tell, want+O+to-infinitive | 76.67% | 2.53 | 3.8 | 1.27 | 3 |
| 100 | Modal auxiliary verb and perfective aspect | 16.67% | 4.00 | 5.26 | 1.26 | 4 |
| 106 | Subjunctive mood (past) | 30.00% | 3.80 | 5.06 | 1.26 | 4 |
| 83 | S+V+indirect object+direct object (if-clause) | 93.33% | 2.63 | 3.88 | 1.25 | 2 |
| 77 | SVC (V=general verb) (C=present participle) | 100.00% | 1.97 | 3.21 | 1.24 | 1 |
| 88 | It+seems+that-clause | 63.33% | 2.73 | 3.94 | 1.21 | 3 |
| 82 | S+V+indirect object+direct object (how-clause) | 83.33% | 2.73 | 3.92 | 1.19 | 2 |
| 102 | Formal object (to-infinitive) | 43.33% | 3.67 | 4.85 | 1.18 | 4 |
| 78 | SVC (V=general verb) (C=past participle) | 76.67% | 3.20 | 4.34 | 1.14 | 3 |
| 107 | Subjunctive mood (past) (I wish~) | 46.67% | 3.57 | 4.69 | 1.12 | 4 |
| 109 | Participial construction (action continuing) | 53.33% | 3.73 | 4.85 | 1.12 | 4 |
| 29 | S+V+indirect object+direct object (how to-infinitive) | 93.33% | 2.40 | 3.47 | 1.07 | 1 |

tended to overestimate their abilities for those items. However, it should be pointed out that, for the questions on these items, the students were given scrambled words and a Japanese expression and told to unscramble these words in order to make an English sentence that corresponded to the meaning of the Japanese expression. Because that type of question was less cognitively demanding, the students might have rated them as relatively easy.

Eleven items belonged to Group 2, where accuracy rates were high, and where the students' difficulty levels were low, but the teachers' levels were high. Table 3.11 shows four typical exam-

**Table 3.9**  *Classification Scheme*

| Groups | | 1 | 2 | 3 | 4 |
|---|---|---|---|---|---|
| | | High accuracy (≧80%) | | Low accuracy (<80%) | |
| Students | Difficulty levels | Low (<3.5) | Low (<3.5) | Low (<3.5) | High (≧3.5) |
| Teachers | | Low (<3.5) | High (≧3.5) | High (≧3.5) | High (≧3.5) |

**Table 3.10**  *Grammatical Items in Group 1*

| No. | Target grammatical items | Answers | Accuracy rates | Students' perceived difficulty levels | Teachers' perceived difficulty levels | Differences (Teachers-Students) |
|---|---|---|---|---|---|---|
| 29 | S + V + indirect object + direct object (how to-infinitive) | I taught him how to send e-mail. | 93.33% | 2.40 | 3.47 | 1.07 |
| 77 | SVC (V=general verb) (C=present participle) | I kept working in a Japanese company. | 100.00% | 1.97 | 3.21 | 1.24 |

**Table 3.11**  *Grammatical Items in Group 2*

| No. | Target grammatical items | Answers | Accuracy rates | Students' perceived difficulty levels | Teachers' perceived difficulty levels | Differences (Teachers-Students) |
|---|---|---|---|---|---|---|
| 80 | S + V + indirect object + direct object (that-clause) | She told me that she had been busy. | 93.33% | 2.07 | 4.15 | 2.08 |
| 84 | SVOC (C=participle) | I saw the man crossing the road. | 96.67% | 2.50 | 4.04 | 1.54 |
| 85 | SVOC (V=causative verb) (C=bare infinitive) | My father made me wait outside. | 86.67% | 2.53 | 4.07 | 1.54 |
| 86 | SVOC (V=sensory verb) (C=bare infinitive) | I saw a lot of people enter the concert. | 96.67% | 2.60 | 4.14 | 1.54 |

ples of items for which the students' difficulty levels scored below 3.00 while the teachers' levels scored above 4.00. These items were all related to sentence patterns. This suggests that, EFL teachers tend to pay much more attention to these items than they actually need. However, it should be mentioned again that questions on these items were also given in the form of having to unscramble the given words to make an English sentence equivalent to a Japanese sentence. The students might have found the items in Group 2 easy to answer because of this type of question used on the grammar test.

Unlike Group 1 and Group 2, Group 3 consists of items for which the students manifested low accuracy rates. For those items, the students' difficulty levels were low, while the teachers' levels were high. Four representative examples of items in Group 3 are displayed in Table 3.12.

For No. 31 and No. 88, the students rated their difficulty levels below 3.00 points; for No. 78 and No. 79, the teachers' difficulty levels exceeded 4.00. Representative errors for each of these four questions are summarized in Table 3.13.

No. 31 is concerned with a seemingly simple sentence pattern, SVOC, which is taught in junior high school but whose accuracy rate did not reach 50%. A typical error made by the students for this question was "You should keep clean this room." Tsuzuki (2003) pointed out that this sentence structure rarely appeared in school English textbooks in Japan; therefore, little input on this structure might have prevented the students from acquiring this item. The other three items were all those taught in high school. In answering No. 88, the students seemed to fail to place a formal "it" as the subject of a sentence. No. 78 involved the use of a past participle. For this question, the students tended to use the past participle "surrounded" to modify a noun phrase "the old man," instead of using it as a complement in the SVC sentence pattern, where the past participle functioned as a part of participial construction. In No. 79, the object of the sentence corresponded to an "if" clause. The students, however, tended to use this "if" clause as an adverbial subordinate clause and to make an interrogative as a main clause, as in "If it stops raining,

**Table 3.12**  *Grammatical Items in Group 3*

| No. | Target grammatical items | Answers | Accuracy rates | Students' perceived difficulty levels | Teachers' perceived difficulty levels | Differences (Teachers-Students) |
|---|---|---|---|---|---|---|
| 31 | SVOC (C=adjective) | You should keep this room clean. | 46.67% | 2.27 | 3.93 | 1.66 |
| 88 | It+seems+that-clause | It seems that she is very happy. | 63.33% | 2.73 | 3.94 | 1.21 |
| 78 | SVC (V=general verb) (C=past participle) | The old man sat surrounded by children. | 76.67% | 3.20 | 4.34 | 1.14 |
| 79 | SVO (O=if-clause) | I wonder if you are free today. | 73.33% | 3.00 | 4.44 | 1.44 |

**Table 3.13**  *Representative Errors for Questions in Group 3*

| No. | Target grammatical items | Japanese prompts | Answers | Typical examples of errors |
|---|---|---|---|---|
| 31 | SVOC (C=adjective) | あなたはこの部屋をきれいにしておくべきです。 | You should keep this room clean. | You should keep clean this room. |
| 88 | It+seems+that-clause | 彼女はとても幸せそうに見えます。 | It seems that she is very happy. | She seems that if is very happy. |
| 78 | SVC (V=general verb) (C=past participle) | その老人は子供たちに囲まれて座っていました。 | The old man sat surrounded by children. | The old man surrounded by children sat. |
| 79 | SVO (O=if-clause) | 君は今日暇かな。 | I wonder if you are free today. | If I wonder are you free today. |

can you come?" This resulted in producing an erroneous sentence: "If I wonder are you free today?" For these items in Group 3, Japanese EFL students need to more consciously analyze the causes of errors they tend to make.

Group 4 was composed of items for which the accuracy rates were low, and both the students' and teachers' perceived difficulty levels were high. Table 3.14 shows three representative items that the students perceived to be difficult, with the scores around 4.00 points, and that teachers considered to be even more difficult, with the scores above 5.00. All of these items were those learned in high school.

Table 3.15 illustrates the correct answers and typical examples of errors for the three items in Group 4.

In answering No. 100, the students had to combine a modal auxiliary verb and the perfective aspect in order to construct the sentence "She must have been extremely angry." However, they failed to use the perfective aspect, producing a simpler sentence

**Table 3.14** *Grammatical Items in Group 4*

| No. | Target grammatical items | Answers | Accuracy rates | Students' perceived difficulty levels | Teachers' perceived difficulty levels | Differences (Teachers-Students) |
|---|---|---|---|---|---|---|
| 100 | Modal auxiliary verb and perfective aspect | She must have been extremely angry. | 16.67% | 4.00 | 5.26 | 1.26 |
| 106 | Subjunctive mood (past) | If I knew her number, I would call her. | 30.00% | 3.80 | 5.06 | 1.26 |
| 108 | Subjunctive mood (past perfect) | If I had had enough money, I would have bought a better computer. | 13.33% | 4.07 | 5.44 | 1.37 |

**Table 3.15** *Representative Errors for Questions in Group 4*

| No. | Target grammatical items | Japanese prompts | Answers | Typical examples of errors |
|---|---|---|---|---|
| 100 | Modal auxiliary verb and perfective aspect | 彼女はひどく怒っていたに違いない。 | She must have been extremely angry. | She must be very angry. |
| 106 | Subjunctive mood (past) | もし彼女の電話番号を知っていれば、僕は彼女に電話するのに。 | If I knew her number, I would call her. | If I know her number, I call her. If I knew her number, I call her. |
| 108 | Subjunctive mood (past perfect) | もし十分なお金をもっていたら、もっと良いコンピュータを買っただろうに。 | If I had had enough money, I would have bought a better computer. | If I had enough money, I would buy a better computer. If I had enough money, I would have bought a better computer. |

that read, "She must be very angry." No. 106 as well as No. 108 were the questions that asked about the use of the subjunctive mood; the former dealt with the subjunctive past while the latter, the subjunctive past perfect. In both questions, the students needed to choose correct verb forms with appropriate tenses in the conditional clauses and the main clauses. For No. 106, the correct verb forms in the conditional and main clauses are "knew" and "would call," respectively. However, some students chose wrong verb forms in both of the two clauses (e.g., "If I know her number, I call her") or in either one of the two (e.g., "If I knew her number, I call her"). Similar tendencies were observed for No. 108, where the correct verb form in the conditional clause was "had had", and the one in the main clause was "would have bought." However, some students could choose the appropriate verb forms for neither of the two clauses (e.g., "If I had enough money, I would buy a better computer), or only one of the two (e.g., "If I had enough money, I would have bought a better computer"). For these items, the students' difficulty levels were high, but not as high as the teachers'. This suggests that it is necessary to raise EFL students' awareness of these items and to encourage them to analyze the errors they are likely to make. The teachers need to provide their students with enough input that contains these structures and enough opportunities to practice using them as output.

## 5.3.2 Grammatical items that the students perceived to be more difficult than did the teachers

Five grammatical items were identified as those for which more than one point difference in difficulty level was observed between the students and teachers. Table 3.16 illustrates those five items, which the students regarded as considerably more difficult than the teachers.

The five items were all those taught in junior high school and are concerned with simple sentence structures. Although they were seemingly easy, the accuracy rates for these items did not reach 80%. Table 3.17 summarizes the correct answers and representative errors for each item.

A notable characteristic common in the results for these five questions was a variety of errors. For example, for No. 42, where the use of the past tense is required, the students used various tenses, such as the past perfect and present perfect. For No. 40, some students did not come up with the adjective "sleepy" or omitted the conjunction "and." For No. 45, the students tended to fail to either choose the correct verb "talk" or use the progressive tense. In answering No. 44, some students used the past progressive tense, while others could not use the past tense of the irregular verb "swim." For No. 6, some students had difficulty with where to put a comma in a sentence. All of these items are dealt with at the beginning stage of EFL teaching in Japan. The teachers, therefore, might have rated the difficulty levels of these items low. However, the students made various

**Table 3.16** *Grammatical Items that the Students Perceived to Be Much More Difficult than Did the Teachers*

| No. | Target grammatical items | Answers | Accuracy rates | Students' perceived difficulty levels | Teachers' perceived difficulty levels | Differences (Teachers-Students) |
|---|---|---|---|---|---|---|
| 42 | Past tense (be verb) | He was in China last year. | 56.67% | 3.30 | 1.98 | −1.32 |
| 40 | Present tense (be verb) | We are tired and sleepy. | 73.33% | 3.73 | 2.44 | −1.29 |
| 45 | Present progressive | My mother is talking on the phone. | 70.00% | 3.17 | 2.06 | −1.11 |
| 44 | Past tense (irregular verb) | We swam in the ocean last summer. | 56.67% | 3.50 | 2.46 | −1.04 |
| 6 | Imperative (affirmative) (general verb) | Walk slowly, please. | 70.00% | 2.67 | 1.65 | −1.02 |

**Table 3.17** *Representative Errors by the Students for the Five Items*

| No. | Target grammatical items | Japanese prompts | Answers | Typical examples of errors |
|---|---|---|---|---|
| 42 | Past tense (be verb) | 彼は去年中国にいました。 | He was in China last year. | He had been in China. He has stayed in China. |
| 40 | Present tense (be verb) | 私たちは疲れていて、眠いです。 | We are tired and sleepy. | We are tired, and sleeping. We are tired, sleep. |
| 45 | Present progressive | 私の母は電話で話しています。 | My mother is talking on the phone. | My mother is calling on the phone. My mother talks. |
| 44 | Past tense (irregular verb) | 私たちは去年の夏に海で泳ぎました。 | We swam in the ocean last summer. | We were swimming in the sea. We swimmed in the sea. |
| 6 | Imperative (affirmative) (general verb) | ゆっくり歩いてください。 | Walk slowly, please. | Please slowly, walk. |

errors in these items and seemed to lack an adequate understanding of them. EFL teachers should be aware that their students still have difficulty with producing sentences that have simple structures taught at the junior high school level.

# 6. Conclusion

The present study attempted to clarify where some similarities and differences between Japanese EFL students and teachers could be observed in terms of their perceived level of difficulty for different grammatical items. Analysis was conducted by considering the students' accuracy rates for these items.

The analysis revealed the following similarities between the students and teachers:

1)  Both the students and teachers tended to regard advanced types of grammatical items taught at the high school level as difficult;

2)  Both the students and teachers tended to consider basic types of grammatical items taught at the junior high school level as easy;

3)  The items with low accuracy rates were likely to be regarded as difficult both by the students and teachers; and

4)  The items with high accuracy rates were likely to be considered easy both by the students and teachers.

The analysis also revealed several differences between the students and teachers:

5)  Generally, the students tended to rate the difficulty levels of various grammatical items lower than the teachers;

6)  There was a group of items for which the teachers underestimated the students' performance; however,

7)  There was also another type of items for which the students overestimated their own performance; and

8)  Typical patterns of errors were observed for these two types of items.

These findings offer several pedagogical implications for EFL grammar teaching for Japanese students at the low-intermediate level. First, some grammatical items taught at the high school level were considered difficult, and their accuracy rates were low; therefore, EFL instructors need to spend a sufficient amount of time teaching these items. Especially problematic items were various relative clauses accompanied by relative pronouns and adverbs. Unlike English, which uses postmodification, Japanese is a language where premodification is used. Such a linguistic difference might be a cause of students' difficulty as well as their errors. The subjunctive mood and a modal auxiliary verb followed by the perfective aspect were also found to be high at the difficulty level and low in accuracy. In the case of the subjunctive mood, correct verb forms with appropriate tenses have to be chosen. Because of such multiple operations required for the subjunctive mood, the students rated this item highly difficult. Careful teaching and much practice might be necessary for the students to overcome these problematic items.

Second, even though the students' average accuracy rate for a total of 110 questions did not reach 80%, the students perceived most of the items as being relatively easier than did the teachers. This result suggests that the students need to carefully reflect on their performance on a grammar test and be fully aware of their present grammatical competence, which can never be said to be satisfactory.

Third, EFL teachers need to differentiate grammatical items that they need to pay more attention to from those that require less attention. The former is a group of items on which the teachers underestimated the students' performance (Group 2), whereas the latter is a group of items on which the students overestimated their own performance (Group 3). For the latter group, in particular, caution is needed, because the students tended to make errors even in simple past-tense sentence patterns taught at the initial stage of English learning, as in "He was in China last year." For those items, close error analysis is called for, and a lot of opportunities both for input and output are required to consolidate the students' acquisition.

The present study has several limitations. The number of students was limited, and their English proficiency was at the low-intermediate level. A larger number of participants with a different proficiency level might have yielded different results. Also, in the present study a composite group of high school and university teachers served as participants, but differences between the two subgroups of teachers were not examined. Because of differences in teaching environments, high school and university teachers might have perceived the same items as difficult or easy.

This study is an exploratory attempt to investigate students' and teachers' perceived difficulty levels of different items taught in junior high school and high school. More attempts are definitely needed to provide richer and more detailed information about where difficulties lie in EFL grammar teaching and learning and what effective instruction could be possible to overcome these difficulties.

# Chapter 4

*Study 3*

# Exploring the developmental stages of EFL students' grammatical competence

## 1. Introduction

Several past studies have attempted to identify which grammatical items cause less difficulty and which cause more difficulty for Japanese EFL students. There are several studies in which Japanese junior high school students served as participants. For instance, Kimura and Kanatani (2006) and Kimura, Kanatani, and Kobayashi (2010) clarified that, for Japanese junior high school students, noun phrases in which nouns are followed by post-modifiers are particularly difficult. Kawamura and Shirahata (2013) and Kawamura (2014) also investigated Japanese junior high school students' performance on the use of different grammatical items, finding that, for these students, pronouns were least difficult while participles were most difficult. There is another group of studies in which Japanese university students participated. Chujo, Yokota, Hasegawa, and Nishigaki (2012) examined Japanese university students' performance on their original grammar test, which included basic items covered in junior high school and high school English textbooks. Chujo, et al. found that the students' overall correct answer rates were below 50%, the sentence structures involving the subjunctive mood and inanimate subject being particularly problematic. Sato, Nakagawa, and Yamana (2007) reported that postmodification still caused trouble even for university students and that the most problematic construction was the noun followed by the present participle.

Compared with the studies in which Japanese junior high school and university students were participants, only a limited number of studies that involved Japanese high school students have been conducted. Most of the studies infer to what extent Japanese high school students have acquired grammatical competence by using the data derived from studies with first-year university students as participants (e.g., Koda, 2011; Nakai, 2011). Furthermore, only a study by Kamimura (2016) attempted to compare high school and university students' performance on a grammar test that contained questions that targeted the same grammatical items. In this study, Kamimura designed a grammar test by utilizing 40 model sentences that had different grammatical items as targets. The sentences appeared in *World Trek* (2nd ed.), an English writing textbook for high school students (Oi et al., 2009). She made a comparative analysis of the high school and university students' accuracy rates for different grammatical items and found some grammatical items that were difficult for the high school students but not difficult for their university counterparts, and also items that were difficult for both the groups of students. Items such as modal auxiliary verbs and to-infinitives belonged to the former group, while inanimate subjects and relative pronouns belonged to the latter. The grammar test used in Kamimura's study included grammatical items and model sentences accompanying those items chosen from that one particular high school EFL writing textbook. The test, therefore, was not comprehensive enough to cover all the grammatical items that are taught in junior high school as well as high school. This means that studies that use a more comprehensive grammar test are needed.

## 2. Purpose of the study

The purpose of the present study was to investigate and trace the developmental stages of grammatical competence of Japanese EFL high school and university students. Four research questions were posited.

1) Which grammatical items do Japanese first-year high school students acquire and which items do they fail to acquire?
2) Which grammatical items do Japanese first-year university students acquire and which items do they fail to acquire?
3) In which grammatical items do the two groups of students differ when accuracy rates are considered?
4) Are there any patterns of errors that characterize the students' developmental stages?

## 3. Procedure

### 3.1 Participants

Two groups of Japanese EFL students were participants in the present study. One group comprised 40 Japanese first-year students at a four-year university who also participated in Study 1 and Study 2. The other group consisted of 122 Japanese first-year high school students. The high school was affiliated with the university, and a number of the high school graduates proceeded to the university every year. Consequently, the two groups of participants were considered comparable enough to deal with the purpose of the study, which was to explore a developmental pattern of Japanese EFL students' grammatical competence.

### 3.2. Data collection

The grammar test the students took is explained in Chapter 1. The university students took the first part of the grammar test in 35 minutes, and after a three-week interval, took the second part again in 35 minutes (see Appendix A). They answered a total of 110 questions on the test, that is, the questions that included as target grammatical items listed on both guidelines, *The Course of Study for Junior High School, Foreign Languages* (MEXT, 2008) and *The Course of Study for High School, Foreign Languages, English* (MEXT, 2010). The high school students, on the other hand, took the test displayed in Appendix C and answered 76 questions that dealt with the items covered in the former guideline, because the remaining 34 items included those that the first-year high school participants had not learned at school. Similar to the university students, the high school counterparts took the first part of the test in 30 minutes, and three weeks later, they took the second part. Because the present study compared the grammatical competence of the high school and university students, the two groups' scores on the 76 questions that appeared on the test for the latter group were subjected to the data analysis explained below.

Following Kamimura (2016), the 76 questions were classified into six categories on the basis of the list of grammatical items described in *The Course of Study for Junior High School, Foreign Languages* (MEXT, 2008): 1) sentences, 2) sentence patterns, 3) pronouns, 4) tense, 5) comparative/superlative, and 6) verb forms.

# 4. Analysis

The high school and university students' answers to the questions on the test were analyzed both quantitatively and qualitatively.

## 4.1 Quantitative analysis

### 4.1.1 Correct answer rates
Each of the high school and university student groups' average accuracy rates was calculated for 1) a total of 76 questions, 2) each of the six different grammatical categories, and 3) each question.

### 4.1.2 Acquisition patterns
Based on the correct-answer rates of the two groups of students, an attempt to search for an acquisition pattern was

**Table 4.1**   *Classification of Grammatical Items Based on 70% Accuracy Rate*

| Groups | High school students | University students |
|--------|----------------------|---------------------|
| 1 | Acquired (accuracy rates≧70%) | Acquired (accuracy rates≧70%) |
| 2 | Not acquired (accuracy rates (<70%) | Acquired (accuracy rates≧70%) |
| 3 | Not acquired (accuracy rates (<70%) | Not acquired (accuracy rates (<70%) |
| 4 | Accquired (accuracy rates≧70%) | Not acquired (accuracy rates (<70%) |

made. Following Brown (1973), Krashen (1977), and Izumi (2002), Kamimura (2016) designated 80% as the threshold level to determine whether or not a given grammatical item had been acquired. All the questions on the grammar test used in this study, however, required the students to unscramble the words to make sentences that corresponded to Japanese sentences. In contrast, the test used in the present study adopted not only this unscramble-words type (34 questions) but also the fill-in-blanks type of questions (42 questions). In the latter type, the students needed to find appropriate words to complete sentences; therefore, it was more cognitively demanding and difficult to answer. Consequently, in this study, 70% accuracy rate was set as a threshold level to determine whether or not a given item had been acquired.

The 76 grammatical items were categorized into four groups: 1) the items that both the high school and university students acquired; 2) those that the university students acquired, but the high school students did not; 3) those that neither the high school nor the university students acquired; and 4) those that the high school students acquired, but the university students did not. Table 4.1 shows the classification scheme.

## 4.2  Qualitative analysis (Error analysis)

Errors made by the high school students were analyzed for the grammatical items in Group 2 and 3. Also, errors made by the university students were examined for the items in Group 3. The error analysis was conducted to investigate possible causes of difficulties for each group of students.

# 5. Results and discussion

## 5.1 Results of quantitative analysis

### 5.1.1 The correct answer rates for the total questions

Table 4.2 shows the high school and university students' correct-answer rates for the 76 questions on the grammar test. Because the questions used in Study 3 were limited to those listed in *The Course of Study for Junior High School, Foreign Languages* (MEXT, 2008), "No." in the first column in Table 4.2 and the subsequent tables does not signify the question number. See Table 1.2 to check which No. corresponds to which question.

The average accuracy rate for the high school students was 58.97%, which was below the 70% threshold level; however, the rate for their university counterparts was 81.40%, which was above 70%. This means that, generally, the university students seemed to successfully acquire the grammatical items they learned in junior high school, whereas the high school students failed to do so.

**Table 4.2** *High School and University Students' Correct-Answer Rates for 76 Questions*

| No. | Grammatical items | Accuracy rates | | |
| | | High school students | University students | Differences |
|---|---|---|---|---|
| 1 | Simple sentence | 75.83% | 96.67% | 20.83% |
| 2 | Compound sentence | 70.00% | 93.33% | 23.33% |
| 3 | Complex sentence | 69.17% | 100.00% | 30.83% |
| 4 | Positive declarative sentence | 79.17% | 100.00% | 20.83% |
| 5 | Negative declarative sentence | 79.17% | 100.00% | 20.83% |
| 6 | Imperative (affirmative) (general verb) | 70.00% | 70.00% | 0.00% |
| 7 | Positive imperative sentence (be verb) | 77.50% | 100.00% | 22.50% |

| No. | Grammatical items | Accuracy rates | | |
|-----|-------------------|----------------|---|---|
| | | High school students | University students | Differences |
| 8 | Negative imperative sentence (general verb) | 75.00% | 100.00% | 25.00% |
| 9 | Negative imperative sentence (be verb) | 70.00% | 100.00% | 30.00% |
| 10 | Yes / no question (general verb) | 79.17% | 100.00% | 20.83% |
| 11 | Yes / no question (be verb) | 72.50% | 100.00% | 27.50% |
| 12 | Affirmative question | 79.17% | 96.67% | 17.50% |
| 13 | Wh-question | 72.50% | 90.00% | 17.50% |
| 14 | SV | 70.00% | 96.67% | 26.67% |
| 15 | SVC (V=be verb) (C=noun) | 78.33% | 96.67% | 18.33% |
| 16 | SVC (V=be verb) (C=pronoun) | 51.67% | 73.33% | 21.67% |
| 17 | SVC (V=be verb) (C=adjective) | 79.17% | 100.00% | 20.83% |
| 18 | SVC (V=general verb) (C=noun) | 79.17% | 100.00% | 20.83% |
| 19 | SVC (V=general verb) (C=adjective) | 74.17% | 100.00% | 25.83% |
| 20 | SVO (O=noun) | 77.50% | 93.33% | 15.83% |
| 21 | SVO (O=pronoun) | 78.33% | 100.00% | 21.67% |
| 22 | SVO (O=gerund) | 72.50% | 100.00% | 27.50% |
| 23 | SVO (O=to-infinitive) | 74.17% | 100.00% | 25.83% |
| 24 | SVO (O=how to-infinitive) | 73.33% | 100.00% | 26.67% |
| 25 | SVO (O=that-clause) | 77.50% | 100.00% | 22.50% |
| 26 | SVO (O=what-clause) | 61.67% | 96.67% | 35.00% |
| 27 | S+V+indirect object+direct object (noun) | 69.17% | 96.67% | 27.50% |
| 28 | S+V+indirect object+direct object (pronoun) | 39.17% | 93.33% | 54.17% |
| 29 | S + V + indirect object + direct object (how to-infinitive) | 65.00% | 93.33% | 28.33% |
| 30 | SVOC (C=noun) | 73.33% | 96.67% | 23.33% |
| 31 | SVOC (C=adjective) | 13.33% | 46.67% | 33.33% |
| 32 | There+be-verb ~ | 62.50% | 100.00% | 37.50% |
| 33 | It+be-verb+(for ~)+to-infinitive | 57.50% | 93.33% | 35.83% |
| 34 | S+tell, want+O+to-infinitive | 40.00% | 76.67% | 36.67% |
| 35 | Personal pronoun (subjective, possessive, objective) | 38.33% | 70.00% | 31.67% |
| 36 | Personal, demonstrative pronoun | 79.17% | 96.67% | 17.50% |
| 37 | Pronoun ('some') | 30.00% | 60.00% | 30.00% |
| 38 | Relative pronoun ('that' as subject) (restrictive use) | 45.00% | 53.33% | 8.33% |
| 39 | Relative pronoun ('which' as object) (restrictive use) | 50.00% | 70.00% | 20.00% |
| 40 | Present tense (be verb) | 48.33% | 73.33% | 25.00% |

| No. | Grammatical items | Accuracy rates | | |
|-----|-------------------|------------------|------------------|-------------|
| | | High school students | University students | Differences |
| 41 | Present tense (general verb) | 55.00% | 73.33% | 18.33% |
| 42 | Past tense (be verb) | 21.67% | 56.67% | 35.00% |
| 43 | Past tense (general verb) | 85.83% | 90.00% | 4.17% |
| 44 | Past tense (irregular verb) | 44.17% | 56.67% | 12.50% |
| 45 | Present progressive | 36.67% | 70.00% | 33.33% |
| 46 | Past progressive | 24.17% | 56.67% | 32.50% |
| 47 | Present perfect (duration) | 54.17% | 73.33% | 19.17% |
| 48 | Present perfect (experience) | 34.17% | 60.00% | 25.83% |
| 49 | Present perfect (completion) | 45.83% | 76.67% | 30.83% |
| 50 | Auxiliary verb (will) (future) | 84.17% | 93.33% | 9.17% |
| 51 | Comparative (adjective) (as ~ as) (as tall as) | 65.83% | 73.33% | 7.50% |
| 52 | Comparative (adjective) (-er) | 71.67% | 96.67% | 25.00% |
| 53 | Superlative (adjective) (-est) | 60.00% | 80.00% | 20.00% |
| 54 | Comparative (adjective) (as ~ as) (as beautiful as) | 67.50% | 73.33% | 5.83% |
| 55 | Comparative (adjective) (more+adjective) | 51.67% | 90.00% | 38.33% |
| 56 | Superlative (adjective) (most+adjective) | 57.50% | 83.33% | 25.83% |
| 57 | Comparative (adjective) (as ~ as) (as good as) | 40.00% | 63.33% | 23.33% |
| 58 | Comparative (adjective) (irregular) | 57.50% | 83.33% | 25.83% |
| 59 | Superlative (adjective) (irregular) | 62.50% | 73.33% | 10.83% |
| 60 | Comparative (adverb) (as ~ as) (as fast as) | 65.83% | 80.00% | 14.17% |
| 61 | Comparative (adverb) (-er) | 61.67% | 86.67% | 25.00% |
| 62 | Superlative (adverb) (-est) | 44.17% | 63.33% | 19.17% |
| 63 | Comparative (adverb) (as ~ as) (as slowly as) | 59.17% | 60.00% | 0.83% |
| 64 | Comparative (adverb) (more+adverb) | 30.83% | 56.67% | 25.83% |
| 65 | Superlative (most+adverb) | 27.50% | 46.67% | 19.17% |
| 66 | Comparative (adverb) (as ~ as) (as well as) | 52.50% | 53.33% | 0.83% |
| 67 | Comparative (adverb) (irregular) | 51.67% | 60.00% | 8.33% |
| 68 | Superlative (adverb) (irregular) | 35.83% | 56.67% | 20.83% |
| 69 | To-infinitive (as noun) | 70.00% | 86.67% | 16.67% |
| 70 | To-infinitive (as adjective) | 45.83% | 50.00% | 4.17% |
| 71 | To-infinitive (as adverb) | 54.17% | 73.33% | 19.17% |
| 72 | Gerund (as object) | 75.00% | 93.33% | 18.33% |
| 73 | Present participle (as adjective) (pre-modification) | 81.67% | 86.67% | 5.00% |
| 74 | Past participle (as adjective) (post-modification) | 34.17% | 73.33% | 39.17% |

| No. | Grammatical items | Accuracy rates | | |
| --- | --- | --- | --- | --- |
| | | High school students | University students | Differences |
| 75 | Passive voice (present) | 30.83% | 70.00% | 39.17% |
| 76 | Passive voice (past) | 13.33% | 43.33% | 30.00% |
| | Average | 58.97% | 81.40% | 22.43% |
| | SD | 0.18 | 0.17 | 0.10 |

## 5.1.2 Accuracy rates for different grammatical categories

Table 4.3 displays the average accuracy rates and their rankings for the six different categories based on the data of the high school and university students.

For all the six categories, the university students' average accuracy rates were above the threshold level of 70%, whereas the high school students' average accuracy rates were below 70% for the five categories. In particular, the high school students had difficulty with pronouns and tenses. Although the high school and university students differed considerably in accuracy rates, the two groups' ranking orders of the accuracy rates were approximately the same.

**Table 4.3**  *Average Accuracy Rates and Their Rankings for Six Different Categories*

| Grammatical cateories | High school students | | University students | |
| --- | --- | --- | --- | --- |
| | Accuracy rates | Ranking order | Accuracy rates | Ranking order |
| Sentences | 74.55% | 1 | 95.90% | 1 |
| Sentence Patterns | 65.12% | 2 | 93.02% | 2 |
| Pronouns | 48.50% | 6 | 70.00% | 6 |
| Tenses | 48.56% | 5 | 70.91% | 5 |
| Comparative/Superlative | 53.52% | 3 | 71.11% | 4 |
| Verb forms | 50.63% | 4 | 72.08% | 3 |

### 5.1.3 Accuracy rates for individual grammatical items: Acquisition pattern

When the 76 grammatical items were analyzed according to the classification scheme displayed in Table 4.1, it was found that no item belonged to Group 4. Therefore, this section reports on the results of the analysis of Groups 1, 2, and 3. Group 1 consisted of the grammatical items for which both the high school and university students reached 70% accuracy, and thus they were called "early-acquired" items. Group 2 included the items for which the university students reached 70% accuracy, but the high school students did not, and therefore, they were regarded as "mid-acquired" items. Finally, Group 3 comprised the items for which neither the high school nor the university students attained 70% accuracy, and thus, they were called "late-acquired" items. When the total of 76 items was categorized into these three groups, there emerged 31 early-acquired, 28 mid-acquired, and 17 late-acquired items. The following sections will discuss the respective groups.

### 5.1.3.1 Early-acquired grammatical items

The majority of the early-acquired items fell in the sentence structure category. As can be seen in Table 4.4, the high school students did not reach 100% for any of the items in Group 1, whereas their university counterparts scored 100% for 15 out of a total of 31 items. The items for which the latter group of students attained 100% accuracy included several types of sentence types (e.g., No. 4, 5, 7, 8, 9, 10, and 11: the positive declarative sentence, negative declarative sentence, positive imperative sentence, negative imperative sentence, and yes-no question) and various types of the SVC (No. 17, 18, and 19) and SVO sentence patterns (No. 21, 22, 23, 24, and 25) where different verbs, complements, and objects were used. This result means that the university students were able to acquire most of the basic English sentence types and patterns, but the high school students still needed more time for practice in order to internalize those items.

**Table 4.4** *Early-acquired Grammatical Items*

| No. | Grammatical items (Early-acquired) | Accuracy rates | | |
| --- | --- | --- | --- | --- |
| | | High school students | University students | Differences |
| 1 | Simple sentence | 75.83% | 96.67% | 20.83% |
| 2 | Compound sentence | 70.00% | 93.33% | 23.33% |
| 4 | Positive declarative sentence | 79.17% | 100.00% | 20.83% |
| 5 | Negative declarative sentence | 79.17% | 100.00% | 20.83% |
| 6 | Imperative (affirmative) (general verb) | 70.00% | 70.00% | 0.00% |
| 7 | Positive imperative sentence (be verb) | 77.50% | 100.00% | 22.50% |
| 8 | Negative imperative sentence (general verb) | 75.00% | 100.00% | 25.00% |
| 9 | Negative imperative sentence (be verb) | 70.00% | 100.00% | 30.00% |
| 10 | Yes / no question (general verb) | 79.17% | 100.00% | 20.83% |
| 11 | Yes / no question (be verb) | 72.50% | 100.00% | 27.50% |
| 12 | Affirmative question | 79.17% | 96.67% | 17.50% |
| 13 | Wh-question | 72.50% | 90.00% | 17.50% |
| 14 | SV | 70.00% | 96.67% | 26.67% |
| 15 | SVC (V=be verb) (C=noun) | 78.33% | 96.67% | 18.33% |
| 17 | SVC (V=be verb) (C=adjective) | 79.17% | 100.00% | 20.83% |
| 18 | SVC (V=general verb) (C=noun) | 79.17% | 100.00% | 20.83% |
| 19 | SVC (V=general verb) (C=adjective) | 74.17% | 100.00% | 25.83% |
| 20 | SVO (O=noun) | 77.50% | 93.33% | 15.83% |
| 21 | SVO (O=pronoun) | 78.33% | 100.00% | 21.67% |
| 22 | SVO (O=gerund) | 72.50% | 100.00% | 27.50% |
| 23 | SVO (O=to-infinitive) | 74.17% | 100.00% | 25.83% |
| 24 | SVO (O=how to-infinitive) | 73.33% | 100.00% | 26.67% |
| 25 | SVO (O=that-clause) | 77.50% | 100.00% | 22.50% |
| 30 | SVOC (C=noun) | 73.33% | 96.67% | 23.33% |
| 36 | Personal, demonstrative pronoun | 79.17% | 96.67% | 17.50% |
| 43 | Past tense (general verb) | 85.83% | 90.00% | 4.17% |
| 50 | Auxiliary verb (will) (future) | 84.17% | 93.33% | 9.17% |
| 52 | Comparative (adjective) (-er) | 71.67% | 96.67% | 25.00% |
| 69 | To-infinitive (as noun) | 70.00% | 86.67% | 16.67% |
| 72 | Gerund (as object) | 75.00% | 93.33% | 18.33% |
| 73 | Present participle (as adjective) (pre-modification) | 81.67% | 86.67% | 5.00% |
| | Average | 75.97% | 95.91% | 19.95% |
| | SD | 0.04 | 0.06 | 0.07 |

### 5.1.3.2 Mid-acquired grammatical items

Table 4.5 displays the high school and university students' accuracy rates for the 28 mid-acquired items.

For 12 items, more than a 30% difference was observed between the two groups of students. The greatest difference (54.16%) was observed in the SVOO sentence pattern (No. 28) where the second object is a pronoun. This was followed by the pattern of the adjectival use of the past participle as a means of postmodification (No. 74) and the passive voice (No. 75), both with a 39.17% difference between the high school and the university student groups. The SVOO pattern, the past participle, and the passive voice themselves are not complicated structures. However, all of these have multiple functions, and the questions asked about the function of each structure that was less familiar to the students. The section on error analysis will discuss what errors were observed for these grammatical structures and why those errors might have occurred.

### 5.1.3.3 Late-acquired grammatical items

Table 4.6 lists the correct answer rates of the two groups for the late-acquired 17 items. For four of the 17 items, neither the high school nor the university students attained more than a 50% accuracy rate. Those items were the SVOC sentence pattern (No. 31), the superlative adverb (No. 65), the adjectival use of the to-infinitive (No. 70), and the passive voice (past) (No. 76). The SVOC sentence pattern is seemingly easy; however, the high school students' accuracy rate for this item was particularly low, that is, 13.33%. One of the possible causes of the difficulty with this item might be a lack of input for the students, because this item seldom appears in junior high school English textbooks in Japan, as Tsuzuki (2003) pointed out. The next sections will explore such possible causes of difficulties for the students by analyzing the errors that they made.

**Table 4.5** *Mid-acquired Grammatical Items*

| No. | Grammatical items (Mid-acquired) | Accuracy rates | | |
|---|---|---|---|---|
| | | High school students | University students | Differences |
| 3 | Complex sentence | 69.17% | 100.00% | 30.83% |
| 16 | SVC (V=be verb) (C=pronoun) | 51.67% | 73.33% | 21.67% |
| 26 | SVO (O=what-clause) | 61.67% | 96.67% | 35.00% |
| 27 | S+V+indirect object+direct object (noun) | 69.17% | 96.67% | 27.50% |
| 28 | S+V+indirect object+direct object (pronoun) | 39.17% | 93.33% | 54.16% |
| 29 | S + V + indirect object + direct object (how to-infinitive) | 65.00% | 93.33% | 28.33% |
| 32 | There+be-verb ~ | 62.50% | 100.00% | 37.50% |
| 33 | It+be-verb+(for ~)+to-infinitive | 57.50% | 93.33% | 35.83% |
| 34 | S+tell, want+O+to-infinitive | 40.00% | 76.67% | 36.67% |
| 35 | Personal pronoun (subjective, possessive, objective) | 38.33% | 70.00% | 31.67% |
| 39 | Relative pronoun ('which' as object) (restrictive use) | 50.00% | 70.00% | 20.00% |
| 40 | Present tense (be verb) | 48.33% | 73.33% | 25.00% |
| 41 | Present tense (general verb) | 55.00% | 73.33% | 18.33% |
| 45 | Present progressive | 36.67% | 70.00% | 33.33% |
| 47 | Present perfect (duration) | 54.17% | 73.33% | 19.17% |
| 49 | Present perfect (completion) | 45.83% | 76.67% | 30.83% |
| 51 | Comparative (adjective ) (as ~ as) (as tall as) | 65.83% | 73.33% | 7.50% |
| 53 | Superlative (adjective) (-est) | 60.00% | 80.00% | 20.00% |
| 54 | Comparative (adjective) (as ~ as) (as beautiful as) | 67.50% | 73.33% | 5.83% |
| 55 | Comparative (adjective) (more+adjective) | 51.67% | 90.00% | 38.33% |
| 56 | Superlative (adjective) (most+adjective) | 57.50% | 83.33% | 25.83% |
| 58 | Comparative (adjective) (irregular) | 57.50% | 83.33% | 25.83% |
| 59 | Superlative (adjective) (irregular) | 62.50% | 73.33% | 10.83% |
| 60 | Comparative (adverb) (as ~ as) (as fast as) | 65.83% | 80.00% | 14.17% |
| 61 | Comparative (adverb) (-er) | 61.67% | 86.67% | 25.00% |
| 71 | To-infinitive (as adverb) | 54.17% | 73.33% | 19.17% |
| 74 | Past participle (as adjective) (post-modification) | 34.17% | 73.33% | 39.17% |
| 75 | Passive voice (present) | 30.83% | 70.00% | 39.17% |
| | Average | 54.05% | 81.07% | 27.02% |
| | SD | 0.11 | 0.10 | 0.11 |

**Table 4.6**  *Late-acquired Grammatical Items*

| No. | Grammatical items (Late-acquired) | Accuracy rates | | |
| --- | --- | --- | --- | --- |
| | | High school students | University students | Differences |
| 31 | SVOC (C=adjective) | 13.33% | 46.67% | 33.33% |
| 37 | Pronoun ('some') | 30.00% | 60.00% | 30.00% |
| 38 | Relative pronoun ('that' as subject) (restrictive use) | 45.00% | 53.33% | 8.33% |
| 42 | Past tense (be verb) | 21.67% | 56.67% | 35.00% |
| 44 | Past tense (irregular verb) | 44.17% | 56.67% | 12.50% |
| 46 | Past progressive | 24.17% | 56.67% | 32.50% |
| 48 | Present perfect (experience) | 34.17% | 60.00% | 25.83% |
| 57 | Comparative (adjective) (as ~as) (as good as) | 40.00% | 63.33% | 23.33% |
| 62 | Superlative (adverb) (-est) | 44.17% | 63.33% | 19.17% |
| 63 | Comparative (adverb) (as ~as) (as slowly as) | 59.17% | 60.00% | 0.83% |
| 64 | Comparative (adverb) (more+adverb) | 30.83% | 56.67% | 25.83% |
| 65 | Superlative (most+adverb) | 27.50% | 46.67% | 19.17% |
| 66 | Comparative (adverb) (as~as) (as well as) | 52.50% | 53.33% | 0.83% |
| 67 | Comparative (adverb) (irregular) | 51.67% | 60.00% | 8.33% |
| 68 | Superlative (adverb) (irregular) | 35.83% | 56.67% | 20.83% |
| 70 | To-infinitive (as adjective) | 45.83% | 50.00% | 4.17% |
| 76 | Passive voice (past) | 13.33% | 43.33% | 30.00% |
| Average | | 36.08% | 55.49% | 19.41% |
| SD | | 0.13 | 0.06 | 0.12 |

## 5.2 Results of qualitative analysis: Error analysis

For the pedagogical purpose for EFL teachers, this section will focus on the mid- and late-acquired items; therefore, error analysis was conducted for the representative items discussed in the previous sections that dealt with the mid- and late-acquired structures.

### 5.2.1 Error analysis for mid-acquired grammatical items

Mid-acquired items were those for which the high school students did not reach the threshold acquisition level of 70%, but the university students did.

The item for which the high school students scored lowest (30.83%) was the passive voice (No. 75).

---

No. 75: 柔道は世界の多くの人々によって楽しまれています。

Answer: Judo is enjoyed by many people in the world.
Target: Passive voice

---

The typical error that the high school students made was "Judo enjoys many people in the world." This suggests that the students failed to differentiate between intransitive and transitive verbs. Another reason might have been that the students seldom encountered the verb "enjoy" in the form of the passive voice; instead, they usually saw this verb in the active voice. For example, in *NEW HORIZON English Course 1* (Sasajima et al., 2012), a junior high school English textbook for the second-year students, this verb appears in the sentences that say, "This is a picture of our school festival. We *enjoy* it very much" (p. 68; italics by Kamimura).

The item for which the students scored second lowest (34.17%) was the adjectival use of the past participle (No. 74).

No. 74: これは多くの学生に読まれている本です。

Answer: This is a book <u>read by a lot of students.</u>
Target: Past participle (adjectival use)

For this item, the students made such errors as "This is a book which read many students," where they unsuccessfully tried to construct the passive voice by using the relative pronoun "which." Another typical error was found in the incorrect sentence that said, "This is a book reading many students." Here the students misused a present participle, "reading," instead of a past participle, "read." No. 74 seemed relatively difficult for the high school students to answer. Actually, for this item, the students needed to tackle two grammatical operations, that is, the passive voice and postmodification, and furthermore, they needed to come up with the adjectival use of the past participle as the form that could realize these two operations. The passive voice is difficult, as was explained in the discussion of No. 75. Postmodification is also difficult for the students because of the difference between English and Japanese. Unlike English, Japanese uses premodification, where the modifying phrases or clauses are placed before the modified words or phrases: The English expression "the book on the desk" corresponds to "*机の上の本,*" where "*机の上の*" (on the desk) modifies "*本*" (the book).

The third item (No. 28) to be analyzed is the one for which a greatest difference in accuracy rate (54. 16%) was observed between the high school students (39. 17%) and the university students (93. 33%). This item concerns the SVOO sentence structure.

No. 28: 彼女にそのことを教えてあげるわ。

Answer: <u>I will show her that.</u>
Target: SVOO sentence pattern

The SVOO sentence pattern itself is commonly found in junior high school textbooks in Japan. However, when a pronoun is used in this pattern, it usually appears either in the position of a direct or indirect object. For example, *NEW HORIZON English Course 2* (Sasajima et al., 2012) includes, as an example model sentence of the SVOO pattern, "Show me your passport, please," where the pronoun "me" is used as an indirect object and "your passport" as a direct object (p. 13). The pattern where both of the objects are pronouns is quite rare, and thus, the students might have been confused with the placement of two pronouns, making a sentence such as "I will show that her."

All of the answers dealing with those three structures are categorized as simple sentences as opposed to compound and complex sentences, according to the school grammar (Yasui, 2003), and therefore, the questions are seemingly easy to answer. However, the results showed the opposite tendency. When used in unfamiliar contexts, the passive voice, postmodification, pronouns, and simple sentences could all be problematic for Japanese EFL students.

## 5.2.2 Error analysis for the late-acquired grammatical items

This section considers some representative late-acquired grammatical items, for which both the high school and university students did not attain more than 50% accuracy rate. The first item was the sentence pattern SVOC in No. 31, in which C was an adjective. For this item, the accuracy rate was 13.33% for the high school students and 46.67% for the university students. Indeed, the former group scored the lowest accuracy rate for this item.

> No. 31: あなたはこの部屋をきれいにしておくべきです。
>
> Answer: You should keep this room clean.
> Target: SVOC pattern (C＝adjective)

Both the high school and university students' erroneous

answer was "You should keep clean this room." The SVOC pattern seldom appears in EFL textbooks for junior high school students (Tsuzuki, 2003); therefore, the lack of input for this sentence pattern might have been the major cause of difficulty for the students. Furthermore, when this pattern appears in a junior high school textbook, a noun or noun phrase, rather than an adjective, is placed in the position of the complement; indeed, an example sentence found in *NEW HORIZON English Course 2* (Sasajima et al., 2012) was "People call it Mt. Taranaki" (p. 124), where the complement was a noun phrase, "Mt. Taranaki."

No. 65 asked about the use of the superlative adverb form. The correct answer rate for the high school students was 27.50% and for the university students, 46.67%; thus, neither of the two groups attained a 50% accuracy rate.

---

No. 65: 彼は家族の中で一番ゆっくり食べます。

Answer: He eats the most slowly in my family.
Target: Superlative adverb form

---

The typical errors found both in the high school and university students' answers were "He eats most slow in my family" and "He eats most slowest." This suggests that both groups did not have a clear idea on how to construct the superlative adverb form. Or as these errors reveal, they mistakenly supposed that the superlative could be formed simply by adding "most" or "-est" to whatever the form of an adverb was. Also, it can be said that the superlative forms of adjectives can be observed more frequently than those of adverbs. If that is the case, then a lack of input for this form of adverb could be a cause of the students' low performance on this grammatical item.

No. 70 involves the adjectival use of the to-infinitive. The high school student group scored a 45.83% accuracy rate, and their university counterparts scored 50.00% for this structure; only a small difference (4.17%) was observed between the two groups of students.

No. 70: 生徒たちはやらなければならない宿題がたくさんあり
ました。

Answer: The students had a lot of homework to do.
Target: Adjectival use of to-infinitive

Examples of incorrect answers produced by some high school students were "The students had a lot of must homework" and "The students had a lot of have to homework." This shows those students' tendency to premodify the word "homework." On the other hand, some university students wrote a sentence such as "The students had a lot of homework they must" or "The students had a lot of homework they should," meaning that those university students made an attempt to postmodify "homework" but failed to do so. However, approximately half of the high school and university students failed to use the to-infinitive as a means of postmodification. Postmodification is a difficult grammatical construction for Japanese EFL learners. Along with the past participle in No. 74 discussed above, the to-infinitive is also a problematic item for the students when it is used as means of postmodification.

The to-infinitive has three major functions: as a noun (e.g., "I want *to drink* water"), as an adjective (e.g., "I had a lot of homework *to do*"), and as an adverb (e.g., "They went to the supermarket *to buy* some food") (*The Courses of Study for Junior High School, Foreign Languages*, MEXT, 2008, pp. 43-44, italics by Kamimura). When the junior high school English textbook *NEW HORIZON English Course 2* (Sasajima, et al., 2012) was examined, it was found that these three functions were introduced in Unit Three in the order of first, the adverbial; second, the nominal; and third and last, the adjectival use. Moreover, when the number of model sentences that used each of the three different functions of the to-infinitive in this Unit Three was counted, the result was that six sentences with the adverbial use, 20 with the nominal use, and only four with the adjectival use were found, respectively. Apparently, in terms of both the order and frequency, the input of this adjectival use of the to-infinitive is scarce, compared with the other functions, especially the nominal function. Here again, a lack of input can be a major cause of the difficulty that the students have with this structure.

Finally, No. 76 asked about the passive voice in the past tense. Both the high school students and university students scored low accuracy rates: 13.33% and 43.33%, respectively.

---

No. 76: この機械はフランスで作られました。

Answer: This machine <u>was made</u> in France.
Target: Passive voice (past)

---

The typical erroneous answer commonly found in the two groups was "This machine (φ) made in France," where a be-verb in the past tense ("was") was missing. This suggests that the students failed to internalize how to construct a sentence in the passive voice, that is, by combining a be-verb and a past participle. Or they might have memorized a phrase such as "made in France" as a formulaic expression and, thus, were not fully aware that "made" is a past participle that could be a component in constructing the passive voice. As is discussed in 4.3.1 in Chapter 2, this question concerned a simple type of the passive voice taught in junior high school. If the students cannot acquire this type, they cannot produce a more complicated type of construction where a passive voice is combined with an auxiliary verb, as in "Mt. Fuji can be seen from Shinjuku." Much attention, therefore, needs to be paid to the teaching and learning of the basic form of the same grammatical item, such as the passive voice, before its advanced form is introduced.

# 6. Conclusion

The present study explored the developmental stages of grammatical competence of Japanese EFL students by examining the high school and university students' scores for the 76 questions on the test compiled according to *The Course of Study for Junior High School, Foreign Languages* (MEXT, 2008). The analysis revealed the following:

1) The Japanese university EFL students reached the threshold level of 70% accuracy on the grammar test that included the grammatical items they had learned at junior high school, both on the whole and for the six different grammatical categories; however,

2) The Japanese high school EFL students reached that level neither on the whole test nor for the six different grammatical categories;

3) Part of the Japanese students' developmental stages of grammatical competence were clarified by identifying the early-, mid-, and late-acquired grammatical items;

4) The mid-acquired items included such items as the passive voice, the adjectival use of the past participle, and the SVOO sentence pattern, which were problematic for the high school students;

5) The late-acquired items included such items as the SVOC sentence pattern, the superlative adverb, the adjectival use of the to-infinitive, and the passive voice in the past tense which both the high school and university students had difficulty with;

6) The analysis of the students' errors found in some of the mid- and late-acquired items revealed characteristic error patterns and possible causes of errors for each item; and

7) The major causes of errors for these items could be accounted for by a lack of input for these items (e.g., the SVOC sentence pattern) and by the differences between English and the students' native language, Japanese (e.g., the adjectival use of the past participle and the to-infinitive).

These findings have several pedagogical implications. First, EFL classroom hours are limited. Therefore, EFL high school teachers need to pay more attention to the mid-acquired and late-acquired items identified in this study, while EFL university teachers need to center their teaching efforts on the late-acquired items.

Second, as the examination of a junior high school textbook demonstrated, the number of model sentences seems to be apparently scarce for some grammatical items, an example of which is the adjectival use of the to-infinitive. It is important, therefore, for EFL teachers to provide their students with more opportunities for input as well as for output in order for their students to internalize the mid- and late-acquired items.

Finally, it is also important for EFL teachers to consider some differences between the target language, English, and the students' native language, Japanese. The students seemed to be confused by the difference between postmodification in English and premodification in Japanese. This could be a possible cause of errors made on the adjectival use of the past participle and the to-infinitive.

The present study has several limitations. The number of participants was limited in this study. A future study that involves a larger number of participants is necessary. Also, only one question was prepared for each grammatical item. Accuracy rates might vary depending on the levels of vocabulary used in questions. Multiple questions for the same item need to be made to confirm the present results. Finally, a study is needed to design grammar instruction targeted at the mid- and late-acquired items by carefully providing students with more opportunities for input and output and by considering differences between English and Japanese. Furthermore, the study should be followed by another study to investigate the effects of such instruction.

# Chapter 5

# Conclusion

This research was conducted with an originally designed grammar test and questionnaire that were comprehensive enough to cover 110 grammatical items listed on *The Course of Study for Junior High Schools, Foreign Languages* (MEXT, 2008) and *The Course of Study for High Schools, Foreign Languages, English* (MEXT, 2010). The research consisted of three studies, each having a different purpose.

Study 1 attempted to clarify how Japanese EFL university students' accuracy rates for the different grammatical items would be related to their perceived difficulty levels of these items. The results of the analysis revealed that most of the grammatical items that the students perceived to be easy but gave incorrect answers to were basic items taught at the junior high school level, while the items that they regarded as difficult and also answered incorrectly were mostly advanced items taught at the high school level. It was also found that the students could not produce advanced forms without being able to produce their basic counterparts in the same grammatical categories, such as post-modification and the passive voice.

Study 2 investigated whether Japanese EFL students' and teachers' perceived difficulty levels of various grammatical items were similar to or different from each other. The analysis revealed both similarities and differences between the two groups' perceptions. As for the similarities, both the teachers and students tended to regard advanced items as difficult and basic items as easy to answer. The items with low accuracy rates were likely to be perceived as difficult, and those with high accuracy rates tended to be considered easy by both the teachers and students. Several differences between the two groups were also observed. Although there was a group of items for which the teachers underestimated the students' performance on the grammar test, the general tendency was that the students overestimated their own performance and that they manifested typical error patterns.

Study 3 explored the developmental stages of Japanese EFL students' grammatical competence. The analysis of the data identified three groups of grammatical items, namely, early-, mid-, and late-acquired items, and these groups could, though partially, give a significant clue to clarifying the Japanese EFL students' developmental pattern. The major causes of errors found in the mid- and late-acquired items could be explained by a lack of input for those items and by the differences between English and the students' native language, Japanese.

From these findings of the respective studies, several pedagogical suggestions could be offered. First, the grammar test designed in these studies could be used in EFL classrooms in Japan so that teachers could have a precise picture of their own students' current grammatical competence. By doing so, the teachers could know which grammatical items their students have difficulty with and which items they do not. Such knowledge would enable the teachers to differentiate the items that they should focus on from those that needs less attention in their teaching.

Second, the teachers need to realize the gap between the students' and their own perceived difficulty levels for different grammatical items. Generally, the students tend to underestimate their difficulty levels and overestimate their grammatical abilities. Therefore, the teachers need to make their students aware of their current grammatical competence and encourage them to engage in the learning of grammar and consolidate their ability with grammar.

Third, Japanese EFL students tend to have difficulty even with the basic types of grammatical items taught at the junior high school level. They cannot produce the advanced grammatical forms unless they can produce the basic types, most of which are categorized as early- or mid-acquired items. Therefore, grammar teaching and learning at the junior high school level is crucial for the students' later solid development of grammatical competence.

Fourth, the grammar test and questionnaire were devised based on *The Course of Study for Junior High Schools, Foreign Languages* (MEXT, 2008) and *The Course of Study for High Schools, Foreign Languages, English* (MEXT, 2010). The new versions of the guidelines were compiled after the present research was conducted: The junior high school version appeared in 2017, and the high school version was published in 2019. Several grammatical items have been added to the new versions, such as the present perfect progressive and S + V + O + bare infinitive structure (as in "I helped my father wash the car") for the junior high school guidelines, and a variety of conjunctions and prepositions for the high school guideline. A more refined and updated grammar test could be designed by referring to those revised guidelines to suit the current needs of Japanese students and teachers.

Last but not least, grammar teaching has recently been deemphasized as a negative reaction to the Grammar-Translation Method. However, grammatical competence is one of the components of communicative competence as defined by Canale and Swain (1980). We should not go back to the traditional Grammar-Translation Method. However, when we think of Otsu's assertion (2012) that students cannot acquire a foreign language unless they learn the grammar of that language, we should reconsider the importance of grammar teaching in Japanese classrooms where English is taught as a foreign language.

# References

Brown, R. (1973). *First language: Early stages.* Cambridge, MS: Harvard University Press.

Canale, M., & Swain, M. (1980). Theoretical bases of communicative approaches to second language teaching and testing. *Applied Linguistics, 1,* 1–47.

Chujo, K., Yokota, K., Hasegawa, S., & Nishigaki, C. (2012). Remedial gakushusha no eigo shujukudo to eigo bunpojuku-tatsudo chosa [Identifying the general English proficiency and distinct grammar proficiency of remedial learners]. *Nihon Daigaku Seisan Kogakubu Kenkyu Hokoku B* [Journal of the College of Industrial Technology, Nihon University, B], *45,* 43–54.

Hashimoto, Y., & Kamimura, T. (2015, August). *Nihonjin daigakusei no eigo bunpo shujukudo chosa: Gakushu shido yoryo ni motozuku bunpo tesuto o mochiite* [An investigation of Japanese university students' acquisition of grammar in EFL: Using a grammar test based on the Courses of Study for Junior High Schools and High Schools, Foreign Languages, English]. Paper presented at the 39th Annual Convention of Kantokoshinetsu Association of Teachers of English. Uenohara, Yamanashi, Japan.

Hashimoto, Y. (2016). *Gakushushidoyoryo ni motozuku nihonjin daigakusei no eigo bunpo noryoku chosa* [An investigation of Japanese university students' grammatical competence in EFL based on the Courses of Study for Junior High School and High School, Foreign Languages, English]. (Master's thesis). Senshu University, Kanagawa, Japan.

Hidai, S., Matsumoto, H., Takahashi, S., Suzuki, A., Oda, M., Enomoto, M., & Tanji, M. (2012). Daigaku nyugaku mae no bunpo no teichakudo ni kansuru kenkyu [A study of pre-college English grammar acquisition]. *Ronso: Tamagawa Daigaku Bungakubu Kiyo* [Bulletin of the Fuculty of Letters,

Tamagawa University], *53*, 31–58.

Izumi, S. (2002). Output, input enhancement, and the noting hypothesis: An experimental study on ESL relativization. *Studies in Second Language Acquisition, 24*, 541–577.

Kamimura, T., & Hashimoto, Y. (2015, November). *Difficulty levels of different grammatical items for university EFL students.* Paper presented at the 25th International Symposium and Book Fair on English Teaching, Taipei, Republic of China.

Kamimura, T. (2016). An investigation of the developmental pattern of Japanese EFL students' grammatical competence. *Senshu Journal of Foreign Language Education, 44*, 65–88.

Kawamura, R., & Shirahata, T. (2013, August). *Chugaku sotsugyosei no eigo bunpo ni okeru konnan komoku no chosa.* [Difficulty levels of English grammatical items for junior high school graduates]. Paper presented at the 37th Annual Convention of Kantokoshinetsu Association of Teachers of English, Matsumoto.

Kawamura, R. (2014). *A study of English grammatical proficiency among junior high school graduates* (Unpublished master's thesis). Shizuoka University, Shizuoka, Japan.

Kimura, M., & Kanatani, K. (2006). Eigo no ku-kozo ni taisuru nipponjin chugakusei no rikaido chosa: "Donyu" kara "teichaku" made no jisa o tokuteisuru kokoromi [A survey on Japanese junior high school students' knowledge of English phrase structures: Identifying time-gaps between instruction and acquisition]. *KATE Bulletin, 20*, 101–112.

Kimura, M., Kanatani, K., & Kobayashi, M. (2010). Nipponjin chugakusei no eigo meishiku kozo no rikaikatei: Judanteki chosa ni yoru jittaihaaku to hanbetsuryoku no kensho [The development of Japanese junior high school students' understandings of English noun phrases: Describing the sequence patterns and testing their discriminative powers]. *KATE Bulletin, 24*, 61–72.

Koda, N. (2011). Rimediaru kyoiku ni okeru bunpo komoku no goto chosa to totatsudo mokuhyo [An error analysis of some grammatical items used in remedial English teaching and its achievement goal. *Shukutoku Tanki Daigaku Kiyo* [Bulletin of the Junior College of Shukutoku], *50,* 225–240.

Krashen, S. (1977). Some issues relating to the Monitor Model. In H. D. Brown, C. Yorio, & R. Crymes (Eds.), *On TESOL '77* (pp. 144–158). Washington, DC: Teachers of English to Speakers of Other Languages.

Ministry of Education, Culture, Sports, Science and Technology. (2008). *Chugakkou gakushu shido yoryo kaisetsu gaikokugo-hen.* [The course of study for junior high schools, foreign languages]. Tokyo: Kairyudo.

Ministry of Education, Culture, Sports, Science and Technology. (2017). *Chugakkou gakushu shido yoryo kaisetsu gaikokugo-hen.* [The course of study for junior high schools, foreign languages]. Tokyo: Kairyudo.

Ministry of Education, Culture, Sports, Science and Technology. (2010). *Kotogakko gakushu shido yoryo kaisetsu gaikokugo-hen.* [The course of study for high schools, foreign languages, English]. Tokyo: Kairyudo.

Ministry of Education, Culture, Sports, Science and Technology. (2019). *Kotogakko gakushu shido yoryo kaisetsu gaikokugo-hen.* [The course of study for high schools, foreign languages, English]. Tokyo: Kairyudo.

Nakabori, A., & Chujo, K. (2004). Bunpo shido ni yoru daigaku level gakushusha no eigo communication noryoku ikusei no koka [Teaching English grammar: Its effects on improving beginning-level college students' communicative pro-ficiency]. *Nihon Daigaku Seisan Kogakubu Kenkyu Hoko-ku B* [Journal of the College of Industrial Technology, Nihon University, B], *37,* 75–83.

Nakai, N. (2008). Dagaku eigo kurasu ni okeru rimediaru kyoiku no kenkyu [A study of remedial education in a Japanese university's freshman English course utilizing English grammar diagnositic tests]. *Meikai Gaikokugogakubu Ronshu* [ Journal, Faculty of Languages and Cultures], *20,* 177–186.

Nakai, N. (2011). Daigaku no ippankyoyo eigo kurasu ni oite bunpo chishiki o ishikika saserukoto no juyosei [On the importance making students conscious of their knowledge of grammar in general-education English courses at Japanese universities]. *Ibunka no Shoso* [Studies in International English Culture], *31*, 133-151.

Oi, K., Kamimura, T., Kumamoto, T., Nix, M., Hagiwara, I., & Matsumoto, K. (2009). *World Trek* (2nd ed.). Tokyo: Kiriharashoten.

Otsu, Y. (2012). Gakushu eibunpo o kangaeru hinto [Some hints on considering pedagogical English grammar]. In Y. Otsu (Ed.), *Gakushu eibunpo o minaoshitai* [Hoping to reconsider pedagogical English grammar] (pp. 2-9). Tokyo: Kenkyusha.

Sasajima, J. et al. (2012). *New horizon English course 1.* Tokyo: Tokyo Shoseki.

Sasajima, J. et al. (2012). *New horizon English course 2.* Tokyo: Tokyo Shoseki.

Sato, T., Nakagawa, T., & Yamana, T. (2007). Daigakusei no eigo gakuryoku chosa—gakushusha wa dokode tsumazukuka— [A study on university students' English abilities—where do learners fail?]. *Bulletin of Tsukuba International University, 13*, 51-68.

Tsuzuki, H. (2003). Koko eigo ni okeru gobunkei shido ni kansuru kosatsu: Aratana bunkeishido no teiji [Consideration on the teaching ways of so-called 'basic five sentence patterns' in high schools: A new way of teaching]. *Journal of the English Literacy Society of Hakodate, 42*, 125-142.

Yasui, M. (2003). *Eibunpo soran* [A better guide to English grammar]. Tokyo: Kaitakusha.

Notes: References in Japanese are written by using Roman letters as the following examples show: 文法 is written as "bunpo," 中学校, as "chugakko," and 研究, as "kenkyu."

# Appendix A

# Grammar test for university students

# 文法テスト1

学籍番号：＿＿＿＿＿＿＿＿＿＿＿＿＿

名　　前：＿＿＿＿＿＿＿＿＿＿＿＿＿

(A)　日本語の意味に合うよう（　）内の語句を並べ替え，文を完成させなさい。
また，それぞれの問題が易しいと感じたか，難しいと感じたか，あてはまる
番号を○で囲みなさい。

　　注意）①選択肢としてカンマ（,）のみが記されていることもある。
　　　　　②文頭にくる語も小文字にしてある。

| | | とても易しい ←→ とても難しい |
|---|---|---|
| 1 | 今朝朝食に何を食べましたか。<br>(you / for breakfast / did / this morning / have / what)？ | 1　2　3　4　5　6 |
| 2 | 彼女は和食と中華料理のどちらが好きですか。<br>(like / or / does / Chinese food / she / Japanese food)？ | 1　2　3　4　5　6 |
| 3 | 私は日本の会社で働き続けました。<br>(in / I / working / kept / a Japanese company). | 1　2　3　4　5　6 |
| 4 | これがあなたの教室ですか。<br>(your classroom / this / is)？ | 1　2　3　4　5　6 |
| 5 | 今日の午後，先生が家に来ます。<br>(to my house / this afternoon / my teacher / will come). | 1　2　3　4　5　6 |
| 6 | 君は今日暇かな。<br>(are / today / I / if / free / wonder / you). | 1　2　3　4　5　6 |

| 7 | 雨が降った時には彼はバスで図書館へ行きます。<br>(goes / he / by bus / when it rains / to the library). | とても易しい ←→ とても難しい<br>1　2　3　4　5　6 |
|---|---|---|
| 8 | 彼は一生懸命英語を勉強しています。<br>(very hard / studies / English / he). | とても易しい ←→ とても難しい<br>1　2　3　4　5　6 |
| 9 | ビルは3匹の猫を飼っています。<br>(three cats / Bill / has). | とても易しい ←→ とても難しい<br>1　2　3　4　5　6 |
| 10 | 彼女は私に忙しかったと言いました。<br>(had been / me / busy / she / that / told / she). | とても易しい ←→ とても難しい<br>1　2　3　4　5　6 |
| 11 | 私たちは彼女が病気だと知りませんでした。<br>(was / that / we / ill / didn't / she / know). | とても易しい ←→ とても難しい<br>1　2　3　4　5　6 |
| 12 | 彼女にそのことを教えてあげるわ。<br>(that / will show / her / I). | とても易しい ←→ とても難しい<br>1　2　3　4　5　6 |
| 13 | トムはスーパーへ行き，彼の妻は家にいました。<br>(his wife / Tom / stayed / , / went / home / and / to the supermarket). | とても易しい ←→ とても難しい<br>1　2　3　4　5　6 |
| 14 | 何が欲しいのか私に教えてください。<br>(what / tell / want / please / you / me). | とても易しい ←→ とても難しい<br>1　2　3　4　5　6 |
| 15 | 彼は医者になりたいと願っていました。<br>(be / hoped / he / to / a doctor). | とても易しい ←→ とても難しい<br>1　2　3　4　5　6 |
| 16 | 学校まで歩いて通っているのですか。<br>(to school / you / do / walk)? | とても易しい ←→ とても難しい<br>1　2　3　4　5　6 |

| 17 | ここで走ってはいけません。<br>(run / don't / here). | とても易しい ⟷ とても難しい<br>1　2　3　4　5　6 |
|---|---|---|
| 18 | 私の父は私を外で待たせました。<br>(me / my father / outside / made / wait). | とても易しい ⟷ とても難しい<br>1　2　3　4　5　6 |
| 19 | あなたはこの部屋をきれいにしておくべきです。<br>(this room / you / clean / should keep). | とても易しい ⟷ とても難しい<br>1　2　3　4　5　6 |
| 20 | こちらが私の先生です。<br>(is / my teacher / this). | とても易しい ⟷ とても難しい<br>1　2　3　4　5　6 |
| 21 | 優子は昨日彼と会いました。<br>(him / yesterday / met / Yuko). | とても易しい ⟷ とても難しい<br>1　2　3　4　5　6 |
| 22 | 彼は本物の冒険家のように思われます。<br>(to / he / a real adventurer / be / seems). | とても易しい ⟷ とても難しい<br>1　2　3　4　5　6 |
| 23 | ゆっくり歩いてください。<br>(slowly, / please / walk). | とても易しい ⟷ とても難しい<br>1　2　3　4　5　6 |

(B)　日本語の意味に合うよう，（　）に語句を補い，文を完成させなさい。
　　また，それぞれの問題が易しいと感じたか，難しいと感じたか，あてはまる
番号を○で囲みなさい。

　　注意）①カンマ（, ）が必要な場合はカンマも含めて記入すること。
　　　　　②（　）内に入る語は1語とは限らない。

| 24 | 私はあなたの両親をスーパーで見かけ，トムは彼らを駅で見かけました。<br><br>（　　　　　　　　　　　） at the supermarket, and （　　　　　　　　　） at the station. | とても易しい ⟷ とても難しい<br>1　2　3　4　5　6 |
|---|---|---|

| 25 | 明日は晴れるでしょう。<br>※（ ）内は3語で<br>It（　　　　　　　　　　　　　　　　）tomorrow. | とても易しい ←→ とても難しい<br>1　2　3　4　5　6 |
|---|---|---|
| 26 | 私達は今日授業でテレビを見ました。<br>We（　　　　　　　　　）in class today. | とても易しい ←→ とても難しい<br>1　2　3　4　5　6 |
| 27 | 私の友人の何人かが私の家にやって来ました。<br>（　　　　　　）of（　　　　　　　　　）came to my house.<br>　　ここは1語で | とても易しい ←→ とても難しい<br>1　2　3　4　5　6 |
| 28 | 私はこのゲームを20回以上やったことがあります。<br>I（　　　　　　　　　　　　　　　　）more than twenty times. | とても易しい ←→ とても難しい<br>1　2　3　4　5　6 |
| 29 | ナンシーは彼女の姉と同じくらい速く歩くことができます。<br>Nancy can（　　　　　　　　　　　　　　　）her sister. | とても易しい ←→ とても難しい<br>1　2　3　4　5　6 |
| 30 | 彼らは食料を買うためにスーパーへ行きました。<br>※that節を使わずに<br>They went to the supermarket（　　　　　　　　　）. | とても易しい ←→ とても難しい<br>1　2　3　4　5　6 |
| 31 | 陽子は日本で一番上手にバイオリンを弾くことができます。<br>Yoko can（　　　　　　　　　　　　　　）in Japan. | とても易しい ←→ とても難しい<br>1　2　3　4　5　6 |
| 32 | この腕時計はあの金色のと同じくらい良いなあ。<br>This watch（　　　　　　　　　　）that gold one. | とても易しい ←→ とても難しい<br>1　2　3　4　5　6 |
| 33 | 私たちはテニスをして楽しみました。<br>We enjoyed（　　　　　　　　　　）. | とても易しい ←→ とても難しい<br>1　2　3　4　5　6 |
| 34 | ボルトは世界で一番速く走ることができます。<br>Bolt can（　　　　　　　　　）in the world. | とても易しい ←→ とても難しい<br>1　2　3　4　5　6 |

| 35 | 健は由実よりも背が高いです。<br><br>Ken（　　　　　　　　　　　　　　　　） Yumi. | とても易しい ←→ とても難しい<br>1　2　3　4　5　6 |
|---|---|---|
| 36 | 由実は太郎と同じくらい上手にピアノを弾くことができます。<br><br>Yumi can（　　　　　　　　　　　　　　　　） Taro. | とても易しい ←→ とても難しい<br>1　2　3　4　5　6 |
| 37 | この機械はフランスで作られました。<br><br>This machine（　　　　　　　　　　　　　　　　）. | とても易しい ←→ とても難しい<br>1　2　3　4　5　6 |
| 38 | 生徒たちはやらなければならない宿題がたくさんありました。<br>※（　）内は3語で<br>The students had a lot of（　　　　　　　　　　　）. | とても易しい ←→ とても難しい<br>1　2　3　4　5　6 |
| 39 | 私の母は電話で話しています。<br><br>My mother（　　　　　　　　　） on the phone. | とても易しい ←→ とても難しい<br>1　2　3　4　5　6 |
| 40 | この絵はあの絵よりも美しいです。<br><br>This picture（　　　　　　　　　　　　　　） that picture. | とても易しい ←→ とても難しい<br>1　2　3　4　5　6 |
| 41 | この車はあの赤いのよりも良いなあ。<br><br>This car（　　　　　　　　　　　　） that red one. | とても易しい ←→ とても難しい<br>1　2　3　4　5　6 |
| 42 | 私たちは毎朝公園を散歩します。<br><br>We（　　　　　　　　　　　　） every morning. | とても易しい ←→ とても難しい<br>1　2　3　4　5　6 |
| 43 | 私たちは疲れていて，眠いです。<br><br>We（　　　　　　　　　　　　　　）. | とても易しい ←→ とても難しい<br>1　2　3　4　5　6 |
| 44 | 由紀は大きくて美しい目をした人形を買いました。<br>※関係代名詞を使って<br>Yuki bought（　　　　　　　　　　　） large beautiful eyes. | とても易しい ←→ とても難しい<br>1　2　3　4　5　6 |

92

| 45 | 私たちがこの本を読むことは重要です。<br>※ to 不定詞を使わないで<br><br>(　　　　　　　　　　) important (　　　　　　　　　　　).<br>　ここは 2 語で | とても易しい ←→ とても難しい<br>1　2　3　4　5　6 |
|---|---|---|
| 46 | 彼らには娘がいました。その娘は音楽を勉強するためにヨーロッパへ行きました。<br>※関係代名詞を使って 1 文で<br><br>They had (　　　　　　　　　　　　　　) to study music. | とても易しい ←→ とても難しい<br>1　2　3　4　5　6 |
| 47 | 彼は 3 時間ずっとインターネットを使っています。<br>※(　) 内は 3 語で<br><br>He (　　　　　　　　　　　　) the Internet for three hours. | とても易しい ←→ とても難しい<br>1　2　3　4　5　6 |
| 48 | 彼女はソウルに旅行しました。そこで彼女は彼女の未来の夫に出会いました。<br>●ソウル= Seoul　※関係副詞（when, where, why, how のいずれか）を使って 1 文で<br><br>She traveled to (　　　　　　　　　　). | とても易しい ←→ とても難しい<br>1　2　3　4　5　6 |
| 49 | 音楽を聴きながら，私は電車の中で本を読んでいました。<br>※(　) 内は 3 語で<br><br>I was reading a book on the train, (　　　　　　　　). | とても易しい ←→ とても難しい<br>1　2　3　4　5　6 |
| 50 | 風邪をひいていたので，寝ていなければなりませんでした。<br>※分詞構文で<br><br>(　　　　　　　　　　　　), I had to stay in bed. | とても易しい ←→ とても難しい<br>1　2　3　4　5　6 |
| 51 | あなたはチャールズがどうやって学校へ来たか知っていますか。<br>●チャールズ= Charles　※関係副詞（when, where, why, how のいずれか）を使って<br><br>Do you know (　　　　　　　　　　)? | とても易しい ←→ とても難しい<br>1　2　3　4　5　6 |
| 52 | 彼女はひどく怒っていたに違いない。<br><br>She (　　　　　　　　　　). | とても易しい ←→ とても難しい<br>1　2　3　4　5　6 |
| 53 | 大切なことは，あなたの心を音楽にこめることです。<br>※関係代名詞を使って，(　) 内は 3 語で<br><br>(　　　　　　　　　　) is to put your heart into your music. | とても易しい ←→ とても難しい<br>1　2　3　4　5　6 |

| 54 | もし十分なお金を持っていたら，もっと良いコンピューターを買っただろうに。<br><br>(　　　　　　　　　) enough money, (　　　　　　) a better computer. | とても易しい ─→ とても難しい<br>1　2　3　4　5　6 |
|---|---|---|
| 55 | 6月に北海道に行きましょう。そのときは天気がいいですよ。<br>※関係副詞（when, where, why, how のいずれか）を使って1文で<br><br>Let's go to Hokkaido in (　　　　　　　　　　). | とても易しい ─→ とても難しい<br>1　2　3　4　5　6 |

## 文法テスト2

学籍番号：＿＿＿＿＿＿＿＿＿＿＿

名　　前：＿＿＿＿＿＿＿＿＿＿＿

(A)　日本語の意味に合うよう（　）内の語句を並べ替え，文を完成させなさい。
また，それぞれの問題が易しいと感じたか，難しいと感じたか，あてはまる
番号を○で囲みなさい。

　　　注意）①選択肢としてカンマ（, ）のみが記されていることもある。
　　　　　　②文頭にくる語も小文字にしてある。

| | | とても易しい ←→ とても難しい |
|---|---|---|
| 1 | 私が英語を理解するのは簡単なことではありません。<br>(for me / English / to / it / easy / is / understand / not). | 1　2　3　4　5　6 |
| 2 | そのジャケット，似合っているよ。<br>(nice / you / in that jacket / look). | 1　2　3　4　5　6 |
| 3 | その老人は子供たちに囲まれて座っていました。<br>(sat / by children / the old man / surrounded). | 1　2　3　4　5　6 |
| 4 | 祖父はコンピューターの使い方を知っています。<br>(knows / how / the computer / my grandfather / use / to). | 1　2　3　4　5　6 |
| 5 | 絵美は野球が好きではありません。<br>(like / Emi / doesn't / baseball). | 1　2　3　4　5　6 |
| 6 | 彼は私にどう感じているかと尋ねました。<br>(I / how / he / me / felt / asked). | 1　2　3　4　5　6 |
| 7 | 机の上のペンは私のです。<br>(mine / on the desk / is / the pen). | 1　2　3　4　5　6 |

| 8 | 健二，静かにして。<br>(please / Kenji / quiet, / be). | とても易しい ←→ とても難しい<br>1　2　3　4　5　6 |
|---|---|---|
| 9 | この試合はわくわくします。<br>(exciting / this game / is). | とても易しい ←→ とても難しい<br>1　2　3　4　5　6 |
| 10 | 私は彼女に暇かどうかと尋ねました。<br>(asked / was / I / she / free / her / if). | とても易しい ←→ とても難しい<br>1　2　3　4　5　6 |
| 11 | その少女はピアニストになりました。<br>(became / the girl / a pianist). | とても易しい ←→ とても難しい<br>1　2　3　4　5　6 |
| 12 | 彼にメールの送り方を教えてあげました。<br>(how / I / e-mail / him / to / taught / send). | とても易しい ←→ とても難しい<br>1　2　3　4　5　6 |
| 13 | メアリーはあなたにこのチョコレートを食べてほしいと思っています。<br>(you / this chocolate / to / Mary / eat / wants). | とても易しい ←→ とても難しい<br>1　2　3　4　5　6 |
| 14 | 私はその人が道路を渡っているところを見ました。<br>(the road / saw / the man / I / crossing). | とても易しい ←→ とても難しい<br>1　2　3　4　5　6 |
| 15 | 私の家の前には古い木があります。<br>(is / in front of / there / my house / an old tree). | とても易しい ←→ とても難しい<br>1　2　3　4　5　6 |
| 16 | えりか，うるさくしないで。<br>(be / don't / noisy, / Erika). | とても易しい ←→ とても難しい<br>1　2　3　4　5　6 |
| 17 | 先生は私たちに面白い話をしてくれました。<br>(us / the teacher / an interesting story / told). | とても易しい ←→ とても難しい<br>1　2　3　4　5　6 |

96

| 18 | 私はたくさんの人々がそのコンサートホールに入るのを見ました。<br>(a lot of people / saw / the concert hall / I / enter). | とても易しい ←→ とても難しい<br>1  2  3  4  5  6 |
|---|---|---|
| 19 | 雨が降っていたので外には出ませんでした。<br>(go out / because / I / it / didn't / was raining). | とても易しい ←→ とても難しい<br>1  2  3  4  5  6 |
| 20 | 私たちは彼を健と呼んでいます。<br>(him / we / Ken / call). | とても易しい ←→ とても難しい<br>1  2  3  4  5  6 |
| 21 | 私たちは給食を食べるのが好きです。<br>(eating / the school lunch / like / we). | とても易しい ←→ とても難しい<br>1  2  3  4  5  6 |
| 22 | 彼女はとても幸せそうに見えます。<br>(that / is /seems / very happy / it / she). | とても易しい ←→ とても難しい<br>1  2  3  4  5  6 |
| 23 | 私は彼が次に何をするか分かりません。<br>(will do / I / what / next / don't / he / know). | とても易しい ←→ とても難しい<br>1  2  3  4  5  6 |

(B) 日本語の意味に合うよう，（ ）に語句を補い，文を完成させなさい。
　また，それぞれの問題が易しいと感じたか，難しいと感じたか，あてはまる番号を○で囲みなさい。

　注意）①カンマ（,）が必要な場合はカンマも含めて記入すること。
　　　　②（ ）内に入る語は1語とは限らない。

| 24 | これが私の一番好きな犬です。<br>※関係代名詞を使って<br><br>This is (　　　　　　　　　　　) the best. | とても易しい ←→ とても難しい<br>1  2  3  4  5  6 |
|---|---|---|
| 25 | 彼はロンドンに2年間住んでいます。<br>※（ ）内は4語で<br><br>He (　　　　　　　　　　　) for two years. | とても易しい ←→ とても難しい<br>1  2  3  4  5  6 |

| 26 | これは私のカバンですが，あのカバンはあなたのです。　とても易しい ←→ とても難しい<br>1　2　3　4　5　6<br>(　　　　　　　　　　　　　　　), but that one is (　　　　　　　　　　). |
|---|---|
| 27 | ジョンはクラスで一番背が高い少年です。　とても易しい ←→ とても難しい<br>1　2　3　4　5　6<br>John (　　　　　　　　　　　　　　) boy in the class. |
| 28 | あの寝ている赤ちゃんを見てください。　とても易しい ←→ とても難しい<br>1　2　3　4　5　6<br>Look at that (　　　　　　　　　　). |
| 29 | ジミーは彼の兄よりも速く泳ぐことができます。　とても易しい ←→ とても難しい<br>1　2　3　4　5　6<br>Jimmy can (　　　　　　　　　　) his brother. |
| 30 | 富士山は日本で一番美しい山です。　とても易しい ←→ とても難しい<br>1　2　3　4　5　6<br>Mt. Fuji (　　　　　　　　　　) mountain in Japan. |
| 31 | 柔道は世界の多くの人々によって楽しまれています。　とても易しい ←→ とても難しい<br>1　2　3　4　5　6<br>Judo (　　　　　　　　　　) in the world. |
| 32 | 私は将来の仕事で英語を使いたいです。　とても易しい ←→ とても難しい<br>1　2　3　4　5　6<br>I want (　　　　　　　　　　) in my future job. |
| 33 | これはこの店で一番良いカメラです。　とても易しい ←→ とても難しい<br>1　2　3　4　5　6<br>This (　　　　　　　　　　) in this store. |
| 34 | 私はジョンと同じくらい背が高いです。　とても易しい ←→ とても難しい<br>1　2　3　4　5　6<br>I (　　　　　　　　　　) John. |
| 35 | 彼は家族の中で一番ゆっくり食べます。　とても易しい ←→ とても難しい<br>1　2　3　4　5　6<br>He (　　　　　　　　　　) in my family. |

98

| 36 | 彼は彼の父と同じくらいゆっくり運転します。 <br> He（　　　　　　　　　　　　　） his father. | とても易しい ←→ とても難しい <br> 1　2　3　4　5　6 |
|---|---|---|
| 37 | 私はちょうど自分の部屋を掃除したところです。 <br> I（　　　　　　　　　　　　　）. | とても易しい ←→ とても難しい <br> 1　2　3　4　5　6 |
| 38 | 彼は去年中国にいました。 <br> He（　　　　　　　　　　　　） last year. | とても易しい ←→ とても難しい <br> 1　2　3　4　5　6 |
| 39 | これは多くの学生によって読まれている本です。 <br> ※関係代名詞を使わずに <br> This is a book（　　　　　　　　）. | とても易しい ←→ とても難しい <br> 1　2　3　4　5　6 |
| 40 | 次郎は花子よりもゆっくり話します。 <br> Jiro（　　　　　　　　） Hanako. | とても易しい ←→ とても難しい <br> 1　2　3　4　5　6 |
| 41 | 私は赤よりも青が好きです。 <br> I like（　　　　　　　　） red. | とても易しい ←→ とても難しい <br> 1　2　3　4　5　6 |
| 42 | 私はその時本を読んでいました。 <br> I（　　　　　　　　） then. | とても易しい ←→ とても難しい <br> 1　2　3　4　5　6 |
| 43 | 私たちは去年の夏に海で泳ぎました。 <br> We（　　　　　　　　） last summer. | とても易しい ←→ とても難しい <br> 1　2　3　4　5　6 |
| 44 | 東京スカイツリーは東京タワーと同じくらい美しいです。 <br> Tokyo Skytree（　　　　　　　　） Tokyo Tower. | とても易しい ←→ とても難しい <br> 1　2　3　4　5　6 |
| 45 | これが私が30年前住んでいた家です。 <br> ※関係副詞（when, where, why, how のいずれか）を使って <br> This is（　　　　　　　　）. | とても易しい ←→ とても難しい <br> 1　2　3　4　5　6 |

| 46 | 私はその問題を解決することは簡単だと思いました。<br>※ to 不定詞を使って<br><br>I found（　　　　　　　　　）easy（　　　　　　　　　　　　　　）.<br>　　　　　ここは 1 語で | とても易しい ←→ とても難しい<br>1　2　3　4　5　6 |
|---|---|---|
| 47 | 先生は私たちを早めに家に帰らせてくれました。<br>※使役動詞を使って<br><br>The teacher（　　　　　　　　　　　　　　）early. | とても易しい ←→ とても難しい<br>1　2　3　4　5　6 |
| 48 | 新しい自転車を持っていればなあ。<br><br>I wish（　　　　　　　　　　）a new bike. | とても易しい ←→ とても難しい<br>1　2　3　4　5　6 |
| 49 | もし彼女の電話番号を知っていれば，僕は彼女に電話するのに。<br><br>（　　　　　　　　　　　　　）her number,（　　　　　　　　）her. | とても易しい ←→ とても難しい<br>1　2　3　4　5　6 |
| 50 | 景気が悪くなると，彼らは仕事を見つけることができませんでした。<br>※（　）内は 3 語で<br><br>When the economy went down, they（　　　　　　　　　）jobs. | とても易しい ←→ とても難しい<br>1　2　3　4　5　6 |
| 51 | 彼女は日本に戻ってくるまで 10 年間ロンドンに住んでいました。<br>※（　）内は 4 語で<br><br>She（　　　　　　　　　　　　）for 10 years before she came back to Japan. | とても易しい ←→ とても難しい<br>1　2　3　4　5　6 |
| 52 | 私はビルが一人でそこへ行ったのは変だと思いました。<br>※ to 不定詞を使わないで<br><br>I found（　　　　　　　　）strange（　　　　　　　　　　　　）.<br>　　　　　ここは 1 語で | とても易しい ←→ とても難しい<br>1　2　3　4　5　6 |
| 53 | 彼は私たちに信頼が大切である理由を教えようとしています。<br>※関係副詞（when, where, why, how のいずれか）を使って<br><br>He tries to tell us（　　　　　　　　　　　　　　）. | とても易しい ←→ とても難しい<br>1　2　3　4　5　6 |
| 54 | 天気がいいと，富士山は新宿から見られます。<br><br>In clear weather, Mt. Fuji（　　　　　　　）from Shinjuku. | とても易しい ←→ とても難しい<br>1　2　3　4　5　6 |

*100*

| 55 | 私は私たちが初めて会った日を覚えています。<br>※関係副詞（when, where, why, how のいずれか）を<br>使って<br><br>I remember (　　　　　　　　　　　　　　　　　　　　). | とても易しい ⟵→ とても難しい<br>1　2　3　4　5　6 |
|---|---|---|

# Appendix B

## Questionnaire for teachers

## 文法項目の難易度に関するアンケートのお願いについて（1）

「中学・高校で学習する文法項目の難易度」について現在研究しております。

つきましては大変恐縮ではございますが，以下のアンケートにご回答いただきたくお願い申し上げます。記入によって得られた必要最低限の個人情報は目的以外に使用することはありません。

---

1．現在教えていらっしゃる学校はどちらですか。該当するものに○をつけてください。

（中学校・高校・大学・その他）

2．何年間学校にお勤めでいらっしゃいますか。　　（教職歴　　　　年）

3．現在の勤務校で使用している教科書名をお書きください。高校の場合は「英語表現Ⅰ」の教科書名をお書きください。

［　　　　　　　　　　　　　　　　　　　　　　　　　　　　　　　］

---

以下の1〜110の問と文法項目を読み，生徒が問に解答することを想定してください。それぞれの文法項目が生徒にとって，どの程度理解するのが易しいか難しいかを考えてください。評価の方法としては，「生徒にとって，とても易しい」と思われる項目は1，「生徒にとって，とても難しい」と思われる項目は6として，該当する番号に○をつけてください。

| | | | とても易しい ←→ とても難しい |
|---|---|---|---|
| 1 | 問 | 今朝朝食に何を食べましたか。(13)<br>(you / for breakfast / did / this morning / have / what)? | 1　2　3　4　5　6 |
| | 文法項目 | **wh-疑問文**<br>What did you have for breakfast this morning? | |
| 2 | 問 | 彼女は和食と中華料理のどちらが好きですか。(12)<br>(like / or / does / Chinese food / she / Japanese food)? | 1　2　3　4　5　6 |
| | 文法項目 | **or を含む選択疑問文**<br>Does she like Japanese food or Chinese food? | |
| 3 | 問 | 私は日本の会社で働き続けました。(77)<br>(in / I / working / kept / a Japanese company). | 1　2　3　4　5　6 |
| | 文法項目 | **主語＋動詞（be 動詞以外の動詞）＋補語（現在分詞）**<br>I kept working in a Japanese company. | |
| 4 | 問 | これがあなたの教室ですか。(11)<br>(your classroom / this / is)? | 1　2　3　4　5　6 |
| | 文法項目 | **yes-no 疑問文（be 動詞）**<br>Is this your classroom? | |

| 5 | 問 | 今日の午後，先生が家に来ます。(1)<br>(to my house / this afternoon / my teacher / will come)． | とても易しい ←→ とても難しい<br>1 2 3 4 5 6 |
| | 文法項目 | **単文**<br>My teacher will come to my house this afternoon. | |
| 6 | 問 | 君は今日暇かな。(79)<br>(are / today / I / if / free / wonder / you)． | とても易しい ←→ とても難しい<br>1 2 3 4 5 6 |
| | 文法項目 | **主語＋動詞＋目的語（if で始まる節）**<br>I wonder if you are free today. | |
| 7 | 問 | 雨が降った時には彼はバスで図書館へ行きます。(14)<br>(goes / he / by bus / when it rains / to the library)． | とても易しい ←→ とても難しい<br>1 2 3 4 5 6 |
| | 文法項目 | **主語＋動詞**<br>He goes to the library by bus when it rains. | |
| 8 | 問 | 彼は一生懸命英語を勉強しています。(20)<br>(very hard / studies / English / he)． | とても易しい ←→ とても難しい<br>1 2 3 4 5 6 |
| | 文法項目 | **主語＋動詞＋目的語（名詞）**<br>He studies English very hard. | |
| 9 | 問 | ビルは3匹の猫を飼っています。(4)<br>(three cats / Bill / has)． | とても易しい ←→ とても難しい<br>1 2 3 4 5 6 |
| | 文法項目 | **肯定の平叙文**<br>Bill has three cats. | |
| 10 | 問 | 彼女は私に忙しかったと言いました。(80)<br>(had been / me / busy / she / that / told / she)． | とても易しい ←→ とても難しい<br>1 2 3 4 5 6 |
| | 文法項目 | **主語＋動詞＋間接目的語＋直接目的語（that で始まる節）**<br>She told me that she had been busy. | |
| 11 | 問 | 私たちは彼女が病気だと知りませんでした。(25)<br>(was / that / we / ill / didn't / she / know)． | とても易しい ←→ とても難しい<br>1 2 3 4 5 6 |
| | 文法項目 | **主語＋動詞＋目的語（that で始まる節）**<br>We didn't know that she was ill. | |
| 12 | 問 | 彼女にそのことを教えてあげるわ。(28)<br>(that / will show / her / I)． | とても易しい ←→ とても難しい<br>1 2 3 4 5 6 |
| | 文法項目 | **主語＋動詞＋間接目的語＋直接目的語（代名詞）**<br>I will show her that. | |
| 13 | 問 | トムはスーパーへ行き，彼の妻は家にいました。(2)<br>(his wife / Tom / stayed / , / went / home / and / to the supermarket)． | とても易しい ←→ とても難しい<br>1 2 3 4 5 6 |
| | 文法項目 | **重文**<br>Tom went to the supermarket, and his wife stayed home. | |

| | | | |
|---|---|---|---|
| 14 | 問 | 何が欲しいのか私に教えてください。(81)<br>(what / tell / want / please / you / me). | とても易しい ←→ とても難しい<br>1 2 3 4 5 6 |
| | 文法項目 | 主語＋動詞＋間接目的語＋直接目的語（whatで始まる節）<br>Please tell me what you want. | |
| 15 | 問 | 彼は医者になりたいと願っていました。(23)<br>(be / hoped / he / to / a doctor). | とても易しい ←→ とても難しい<br>1 2 3 4 5 6 |
| | 文法項目 | 主語＋動詞＋目的語（to不定詞）<br>He hoped to be a doctor. | |
| 16 | 問 | 学校まで歩いて通っているのですか。(10)<br>(to school / you / do / walk)? | とても易しい ←→ とても難しい<br>1 2 3 4 5 6 |
| | 文法項目 | yes-no疑問文（一般動詞）<br>Do you walk to school? | |
| 17 | 問 | ここで走ってはいけません。(8)<br>(run / don't / here). | とても易しい ←→ とても難しい<br>1 2 3 4 5 6 |
| | 文法項目 | 否定の命令文（一般動詞）<br>Don't run here. | |
| 18 | 問 | 私の父は私を外で待たせました。(85)<br>(me / my father / outside / made / wait). | とても易しい ←→ とても難しい<br>1 2 3 4 5 6 |
| | 文法項目 | 主語＋動詞（使役動詞）＋目的語＋補語（原形不定詞）<br>My father made me wait outside. | |
| 19 | 問 | あなたはこの部屋をきれいにしておくべきです。(31)<br>(this room / you / clean / should keep). | とても易しい ←→ とても難しい<br>1 2 3 4 5 6 |
| | 文法項目 | 主語＋動詞＋目的語＋補語（形容詞）<br>You should keep this room clean. | |
| 20 | 問 | こちらが私の先生です。(15)<br>(is / my teacher / this). | とても易しい ←→ とても難しい<br>1 2 3 4 5 6 |
| | 文法項目 | 主語＋動詞（be動詞）＋補語（名詞）<br>This is my teacher. | |
| 21 | 問 | 優子は昨日彼と会いました。(21)<br>(him / yesterday / met / Yuko). | とても易しい ←→ とても難しい<br>1 2 3 4 5 6 |
| | 文法項目 | 主語＋動詞＋目的語（代名詞）<br>Yuko met him yesterday. | |
| 22 | 問 | 彼は本物の冒険家のように思われます。(87)<br>(to / he / a real adventurer / be / seems). | とても易しい ←→ とても難しい<br>1 2 3 4 5 6 |
| | 文法項目 | 主語＋seem＋to不定詞<br>He seems to be a real adventurer. | |
| 23 | 問 | ゆっくり歩いてください。(6)<br>(slowly, / please / walk). | とても易しい ←→ とても難しい<br>1 2 3 4 5 6 |
| | 文法項目 | 肯定の命令文（一般動詞）<br>Walk slowly, please. | |

| 24 | 問 | 私はあなたの両親をスーパーで見かけ，トムは彼らを駅で見かけました。(35)<br>(　　　　　　　) at the supermarket, and (　　　　　　　) at the station. | とても易しい ←→ とても難しい<br>1　2　3　4　5　6 |
|---|---|---|---|
| | 文法項目 | 人称代名詞（主格・所有格・目的格）<br>I saw your parents at the supermarket, and Tom saw them at the station. | |
| 25 | 問 | 明日は晴れるでしょう。(50)　※(　) 内は3語で<br>It (　　　　　　　) tomorrow. | とても易しい ←→ とても難しい<br>1　2　3　4　5　6 |
| | 文法項目 | 助動詞を用いた未来表現<br>It will be fine tomorrow. | |
| 26 | 問 | 私達は今日授業でテレビを見ました。(43)<br>We (　　　　　　　) in class today. | とても易しい ←→ とても難しい<br>1　2　3　4　5　6 |
| | 文法項目 | 過去形（一般動詞）<br>We watched TV in class today. | |
| 27 | 問 | 私の友人の何人かが私の家にやって来ました。(37)<br>(　　　　　) of (　　　　　)<br>came to my house. | とても易しい ←→ とても難しい<br>1　2　3　4　5　6 |
| | 文法項目 | 数量代名詞（some）<br>Some of my friends came to my house. | |
| 28 | 問 | 私はこのゲームを20回以上やったことがあります。(48)<br>I (　　　　　　　)<br>more than twenty times. | とても易しい ←→ とても難しい<br>1　2　3　4　5　6 |
| | 文法項目 | 現在完了形（経験）<br>I have played this game more than twenty times. | |
| 29 | 問 | ナンシーは彼女の姉と同じくらい速く歩くことができます。(60)<br>Nancy can (　　　　　　　) her sister. | とても易しい ←→ とても難しい<br>1　2　3　4　5　6 |
| | 文法項目 | 副詞の原級による比較<br>Nancy can walk as fast as her sister. | |
| 30 | 問 | 彼らは食料を買うためにスーパーへ行きました。(71)<br>※ that 節を使わずに<br>They went to the supermarket (　　　　). | とても易しい ←→ とても難しい<br>1　2　3　4　5　6 |
| | 文法項目 | to 不定詞（副詞的用法）<br>They went to the supermarket to buy some food. | |

| 31 | 問 | 陽子は日本で一番上手にバイオリンを弾くことができます。(68)<br>Yoko can (　　　　　　　　　　　) in Japan. | とても易しい ←→ とても難しい<br>1 2 3 4 5 6 |
| | 文法<br>項目 | 副詞の最上級（不規則変化）<br>Yoko can play the violin the best in Japan. | |
| 32 | 問 | この腕時計はあの金色のと同じくらい良いなあ。(57)<br>This watch (　　　　　　　　　　) that gold one. | とても易しい ←→ とても難しい<br>1 2 3 4 5 6 |
| | 文法<br>項目 | 形容詞の原級による比較（不規則変化）<br>This watch is as good as that gold one. | |
| 33 | 問 | 私たちはテニスをして楽しみました。(72)　※（ ）内は2語で<br>We enjoyed (　　　　　　　　　　). | とても易しい ←→ とても難しい<br>1 2 3 4 5 6 |
| | 文法<br>項目 | 動名詞（動詞の目的語）<br>We enjoyed playing tennis. | |
| 34 | 問 | ボルトは世界で一番速く走ることができます。(62)<br>Bolt can (　　　　　　　　) in the world. | とても易しい ←→ とても難しい<br>1 2 3 4 5 6 |
| | 文法<br>項目 | 副詞の最上級（-est）<br>Bolt can run fastest in the world. | |
| 35 | 問 | 健は由実よりも背が高いです。(52)<br>Ken (　　　　　　　　　　) Yumi. | とても易しい ←→ とても難しい<br>1 2 3 4 5 6 |
| | 文法<br>項目 | 形容詞の比較級（-er）<br>Ken is taller than Yumi. | |
| 36 | 問 | 由実は太郎と同じくらい上手にピアノを弾くことができます。(66)<br>Yumi can (　　　　　　　　　) Taro. | とても易しい ←→ とても難しい<br>1 2 3 4 5 6 |
| | 文法<br>項目 | 副詞の原級による比較（不規則変化）<br>Yumi can play the piano as well as Taro. | |
| 37 | 問 | この機械はフランスで作られました。(76)<br>This machine (　　　　　　　　). | とても易しい ←→ とても難しい<br>1 2 3 4 5 6 |
| | 文法<br>項目 | 受け身（過去形）<br>This machine was made in France. | |
| 38 | 問 | 生徒たちはやらなければならない宿題がたくさんありました。(70)　※（ ）内は3語で<br>The students had a lot of<br>(　　　　　　　　　　). | とても易しい ←→ とても難しい<br>1 2 3 4 5 6 |
| | 文法<br>項目 | to 不定詞（形容詞的用法）<br>The students had a lot of homework to do. | |

| 47 | 問 | 彼は3時間ずっとインターネットを使っています。(104) ※（ ）内は3語で<br>He （                    ) the Internet for three hours. | とても易しい ⟵⟶ とても難しい<br>1 2 3 4 5 6 |
| | 文法項目 | **現在完了進行形**<br>He has been using the Internet for three hours. | |
| 48 | 問 | 彼女はソウルに旅行しました。そこで彼女は彼女の未来の夫に出会いました。(96) ※関係副詞を使って1文で<br>She traveled to （                    ). | とても易しい ⟵⟶ とても難しい<br>1 2 3 4 5 6 |
| | 文法項目 | **関係副詞（where の非制限的用法）**<br>She traveled to Seoul, where she met her future husband. | |
| 49 | 問 | 音楽を聴きながら，私は電車の中で本を読んでいました。(109) ※（ ）内は3語で<br>I was reading a book on the train, （                    ). | とても易しい ⟵⟶ とても難しい<br>1 2 3 4 5 6 |
| | 文法項目 | **分詞構文（付帯状況）**<br>I was reading a book on the train, listening to music. | |
| 50 | 問 | 風邪をひいていたので，寝ていなければなりませんでした。(110) ※分詞構文で<br>（                    ), I had to stay in bed. | とても易しい ⟵⟶ とても難しい<br>1 2 3 4 5 6 |
| | 文法項目 | **分詞構文（理由）**<br>Having a cold, I had to stay in bed. | |
| 51 | 問 | あなたはチャールズがどうやって学校へ来たか知っていますか。(95) ※関係副詞を使って<br>Do you know （                    )? | とても易しい ⟵⟶ とても難しい<br>1 2 3 4 5 6 |
| | 文法項目 | **関係副詞（how）**<br>Do you know how Charles came to school? | |
| 52 | 問 | 彼女はひどく怒っていたに違いない。(100)<br>She （                    ). | とても易しい ⟵⟶ とても難しい<br>1 2 3 4 5 6 |
| | 文法項目 | **助動詞と完了形を用いた過去に関する推測の表現**<br>She must have been extremely angry. | |

| | | | とても易しい ←→ とても難しい |
|---|---|---|---|
| 53 | 問 | 大切なことは，あなたの心を音楽にこめることです。<br>(90)　※関係代名詞を使って，（　）内は 3 語で<br>（　　　　　　　　　　　　　　　　） is to put<br>your heart into your music. | 1　2　3　4　5　6 |
| | 文法項目 | 関係代名詞（what）<br><u>What is important</u> is to put your heart into your<br>music. | |
| 54 | 問 | もし十分なお金を持っていたら，もっと良いコンピューターを買っただろうに。(108)<br>（　　　　　　　　　） enough money,<br>（　　　　　　　　　　　） a better computer. | とても易しい ←→ とても難しい<br>1　2　3　4　5　6 |
| | 文法項目 | 仮定法過去完了<br>If I <u>had had</u> enough money, <u>I would have bought</u><br>a better computer. | |
| 55 | 問 | 6 月に北海道に行きましょう。そのときは天気がいいですよ。(97)　※関係副詞を使って 1 文で<br>Let's go to Hokkaido in（　　　　　　　　　　　　　　　）. | とても易しい ←→ とても難しい<br>1　2　3　4　5　6 |
| | 文法項目 | 関係副詞（when の非制限的用法）<br>Let's go to Hokkaido in <u>June, when the weather is</u><br><u>beautiful.</u> | |

## 文法項目の難易度に関するアンケートのお願いについて (2)

| 56 | 問 | 私が英語を理解するのは簡単なことではありません。(33)<br>(for me / English / to / it / easy / is / understand / not). | とても易しい ←→ とても難しい<br>1　2　3　4　5　6 |
|---|---|---|---|
| | 文法項目 | it＋be 動詞＋〜 (＋for〜) ＋to 不定詞<br>It is not easy for me to understand English. | |
| 57 | 問 | そのジャケット，似合っているよ。(19)<br>(nice / you / in that jacket / look). | とても易しい ←→ とても難しい<br>1　2　3　4　5　6 |
| | 文法項目 | 主語＋動詞 (be 動詞以外の動詞) ＋補語 (形容詞)<br>You look nice in that jacket. | |
| 58 | 問 | その老人は子供たちに囲まれて座っていました。(78)<br>(sat / by children / the old man / surrounded). | とても易しい ←→ とても難しい<br>1　2　3　4　5　6 |
| | 文法項目 | 主語＋動詞 (be 動詞以外の動詞) ＋補語 (過去分詞)<br>The old man sat surrounded by children. | |
| 59 | 問 | 祖父はコンピューターの使い方を知っています。(24)<br>(knows / how / the computer / my grandfather / use / to). | とても易しい ←→ とても難しい<br>1　2　3　4　5　6 |
| | 文法項目 | 主語＋動詞＋目的語 (how to 不定詞)<br>My grandfather knows how to use the computer. | |
| 60 | 問 | 絵美は野球が好きではありません。(5)<br>(like / Emi / doesn't / baseball). | とても易しい ←→ とても難しい<br>1　2　3　4　5　6 |
| | 文法項目 | 否定の平叙文<br>Emi doesn't like baseball. | |
| 61 | 問 | 彼は私にどう感じているかと尋ねました。(82)<br>(I / how / he / me / felt / asked). | とても易しい ←→ とても難しい<br>1　2　3　4　5　6 |
| | 文法項目 | 主語＋動詞＋間接目的語＋直接目的語 (how で始まる節)<br>He asked me how I felt. | |
| 62 | 問 | 机の上のペンは私のです。(16)<br>(mine / on the desk / is / the pen). | とても易しい ←→ とても難しい<br>1　2　3　4　5　6 |
| | 文法項目 | 主語＋動詞 (be 動詞) ＋補語 (代名詞)<br>The pen on the desk is mine. | |
| 63 | 問 | 健二，静かにして。(7)<br>(please / Kenji / quiet, / be). | とても易しい ←→ とても難しい<br>1　2　3　4　5　6 |
| | 文法項目 | 肯定の命令文 (be 動詞)<br>Please be quiet, Kenji. | |

| 64 | 問 | この試合はわくわくします。（17）<br>(exciting / this game / is). | とても易しい ←→ とても難しい<br>1 2 3 4 5 6 |
| | 文法項目 | 主語＋動詞（be 動詞）＋補語（形容詞）<br>This game is exciting. | |
| 65 | 問 | 私は彼女に暇かどうかと尋ねました。（83）<br>(asked / was / I / she / free / her / if). | とても易しい ←→ とても難しい<br>1 2 3 4 5 6 |
| | 文法項目 | 主語＋動詞＋間接目的語＋直接目的語（if で始まる節）<br>I asked her if she was free. | |
| 66 | 問 | その少女はピアニストになりました。（18）<br>(became / the girl / a pianist). | とても易しい ←→ とても難しい<br>1 2 3 4 5 6 |
| | 文法項目 | 主語＋動詞（be 動詞以外の動詞）＋補語（名詞）<br>The girl became a pianist. | |
| 67 | 問 | 彼にメールの送り方を教えてあげました。（29）<br>(how / I / e-mail / him / to / taught / send). | とても易しい ←→ とても難しい<br>1 2 3 4 5 6 |
| | 文法項目 | 主語＋動詞＋間接目的語＋直接目的語（how to 不定詞）<br>I taught him how to send e-mail. | |
| 68 | 問 | メアリーはあなたにこのチョコレートを食べてほしいと思っています。（34）<br>(you / this chocolate / to / Mary / eat / wants). | とても易しい ←→ とても難しい<br>1 2 3 4 5 6 |
| | 文法項目 | 主語＋tell，want など＋目的語＋to 不定詞<br>Mary wants you to eat this chocolate. | |
| 69 | 問 | 私はその人が道路を渡っているところを見ました。（84）<br>(the road / saw / the man / I / crossing). | とても易しい ←→ とても難しい<br>1 2 3 4 5 6 |
| | 文法項目 | 主語＋動詞＋目的語＋補語（分詞）<br>I saw the man crossing the road. | |
| 70 | 問 | 私の家の前には古い木があります。（32）<br>(is / in front of / there / my house / an old tree). | とても易しい ←→ とても難しい<br>1 2 3 4 5 6 |
| | 文法項目 | There＋be 動詞＋〜<br>There is an old tree in front of my house. | |
| 71 | 問 | えりか，うるさくしないで。（9）<br>(be / don't / noisy, / Erika). | とても易しい ←→ とても難しい<br>1 2 3 4 5 6 |
| | 文法項目 | 否定の命令文（be 動詞）<br>Don't be noisy, Erika. | |
| 72 | 問 | 先生は私たちに面白い話をしてくれました。（27）<br>(us / the teacher / an interesting story / told). | とても易しい ←→ とても難しい<br>1 2 3 4 5 6 |
| | 文法項目 | 主語＋動詞＋間接目的語＋直接目的語（名詞）<br>The teacher told us an interesting story. | |

| 73 | 問 | 私はたくさんの人々がそのコンサートホールに入るのを見ました。(86)<br>(a lot of people / saw / the concert hall / I / enter). | とても易しい ←→ とても難しい<br>1　2　3　4　5　6 |
|---|---|---|---|
| | 文法項目 | 主語＋動詞（知覚動詞）＋目的語＋補語（原形不定詞）<br>I saw a lot of people enter the concert hall. | |
| 74 | 問 | 雨が降っていたので外には出ませんでした。(3)<br>(go out / because / I / it / didn't / was raining). | とても易しい ←→ とても難しい<br>1　2　3　4　5　6 |
| | 文法項目 | 複文<br>I didn't go out because it was raining. | |
| 75 | 問 | 私たちは彼を健と呼んでいます。(30)<br>(him / we / Ken / call). | とても易しい ←→ とても難しい<br>1　2　3　4　5　6 |
| | 文法項目 | 主語＋動詞＋目的語＋補語（名詞）<br>We call him Ken. | |
| 76 | 問 | 私たちは給食を食べるのが好きです。(22)<br>(eating / the school lunch / like / we). | とても易しい ←→ とても難しい<br>1　2　3　4　5　6 |
| | 文法項目 | 主語＋動詞＋目的語（動名詞）<br>We like eating the school lunch. | |
| 77 | 問 | 彼女はとても幸せそうに見えます。(88)<br>(that / is /seems / very happy / it / she). | とても易しい ←→ とても難しい<br>1　2　3　4　5　6 |
| | 文法項目 | It＋seem＋that で始まる節<br>It seems that she is very happy. | |
| 78 | 問 | 私は彼が次に何をするか分かりません。(26)<br>(will do / I / what / next / don't / he / know). | とても易しい ←→ とても難しい<br>1　2　3　4　5　6 |
| | 文法項目 | 主語＋動詞＋目的語（what で始まる節）<br>I don't know what he will do next. | |

| 79 | 問 | これが私の一番好きな犬です。(39)　※関係代名詞を使って<br>This is (　　　　　　　　　　　) the best. | とても易しい ←→ とても難しい<br>1　2　3　4　5　6 |
|---|---|---|---|
| | 文法項目 | 関係代名詞：目的格の which（制限的用法）<br>This is the dog which I like the best. | |
| 80 | 問 | 彼はロンドンに2年間住んでいます。(47)　※（ ）内は4語で<br>He (　　　　　　　　　) for two years. | とても易しい ←→ とても難しい<br>1　2　3　4　5　6 |
| | 文法項目 | 現在完了形（継続）<br>He has lived in London for two years. | |

*114*

| | | | とても易しい ←→ とても難しい |
|---|---|---|---|
| 81 | 問 | これは私のカバンですが，あのカバンはあなたのです。(36)<br>(　　　　　　　　　　　　　　　), but that one is (　　　　　　　　). | 1　2　3　4　5　6 |
| | 文法項目 | 人称・指示代名詞<br>This is my bag, but that one is yours. | |
| 82 | 問 | ジョンはクラスで一番背が高い少年です。(53)<br>John (　　　　　　　　　　　　) boy in the class. | 1　2　3　4　5　6 |
| | 文法項目 | 形容詞の最上級（-est）<br>John is the tallest boy in the class. | |
| 83 | 問 | あの寝ている赤ちゃんを見てください。(73)<br>Look at that (　　　　　　　　　). | 1　2　3　4　5　6 |
| | 文法項目 | 現在分詞の形容詞としての用法（前置修飾）<br>Look at that sleeping baby. | |
| 84 | 問 | ジミーは彼の兄よりも速く泳ぐことができます。(61)<br>Jimmy can (　　　　　　　　) his brother. | 1　2　3　4　5　6 |
| | 文法項目 | 副詞の比較級（-er）<br>Jimmy can swim faster than his brother. | |
| 85 | 問 | 富士山は日本で一番美しい山です。(56)<br>Mt. Fuji (　　　　　　　　　) mountain in Japan. | 1　2　3　4　5　6 |
| | 文法項目 | 形容詞の最上級（most＋形容詞）<br>Mt. Fuji is the most beautiful mountain in Japan. | |
| 86 | 問 | 柔道は世界の多くの人々によって楽しまれています。(75)<br>Judo (　　　　　　　　) in the world. | 1　2　3　4　5　6 |
| | 文法項目 | 受け身（現在形）<br>Judo is enjoyed by many people in the world. | |
| 87 | 問 | 私は将来の仕事で英語を使いたいです。(69)<br>I want (　　　　　　　　) in my future job. | 1　2　3　4　5　6 |
| | 文法項目 | to 不定詞（名詞的用法）<br>I want to use English in my future job. | |
| 88 | 問 | これはこの店で一番良いカメラです。(59)<br>This (　　　　　　　　) in this store. | 1　2　3　4　5　6 |
| | 文法項目 | 形容詞の最上級（不規則変化）<br>This is the best camera in this store. | |

| 89 | 問 | 私はジョンと同じくらい背が高いです。(51)<br>I (　　　　　　　　　　　　　　) John. | とても易しい ←→ とても難しい<br>1　2　3　4　5　6 |
|---|---|---|---|
| | 文法項目 | 形容詞の原級による比較<br>I am as tall as John. | |
| 90 | 問 | 彼は家族の中で一番ゆっくり食べます。(65)<br>He (　　　　　　　　　　　　　　) in my family. | とても易しい ←→ とても難しい<br>1　2　3　4　5　6 |
| | 文法項目 | 副詞の最上級（most＋副詞）<br>He eats the most slowly in my family. | |
| 91 | 問 | 彼は彼の父と同じくらいゆっくり運転します。(63)<br>He (　　　　　　　　　　　　　　) his father. | とても易しい ←→ とても難しい<br>1　2　3　4　5　6 |
| | 文法項目 | 副詞の原級による比較<br>He drives as slowly as his father. | |
| 92 | 問 | 私はちょうど自分の部屋を掃除したところです。(49)<br>I (　　　　　　　　　　　　　　). | とても易しい ←→ とても難しい<br>1　2　3　4　5　6 |
| | 文法項目 | 現在完了形（完了）<br>I have just cleaned my room. | |
| 93 | 問 | 彼は去年中国にいました。(42)<br>He (　　　　　　　　　　　　　　) last year. | とても易しい ←→ とても難しい<br>1　2　3　4　5　6 |
| | 文法項目 | 過去形（be 動詞）<br>He was in China last year. | |
| 94 | 問 | これは多くの学生によって読まれている本です。(74)<br>This is a book (　　　　　　　　　　　　). | とても易しい ←→ とても難しい<br>1　2　3　4　5　6 |
| | 文法項目 | 過去分詞の形容詞としての用法（後置修飾）<br>This is a book read by a lot of students. | |
| 95 | 問 | 次郎は花子よりもゆっくり話します。(64)<br>Jiro (　　　　　　　　　　　　　) Hanako. | とても易しい ←→ とても難しい<br>1　2　3　4　5　6 |
| | 文法項目 | 副詞の比較級（more＋副詞）<br>Jiro speaks more slowly than Hanako. | |
| 96 | 問 | 私は赤よりも青が好きです。(67)<br>I like (　　　　　　　　　　　　　) red. | とても易しい ←→ とても難しい<br>1　2　3　4　5　6 |
| | 文法項目 | 副詞の比較級（不規則変化）<br>I like blue better than red. | |
| 97 | 問 | 私はその時本を読んでいました。(46)<br>I (　　　　　　　　　　　　　) then. | とても易しい ←→ とても難しい<br>1　2　3　4　5　6 |
| | 文法項目 | 過去進行形<br>I was reading a book then. | |
| 98 | 問 | 私たちは去年の夏に海で泳ぎました。(44)<br>We (　　　　　　　　　　　　) last summer. | とても易しい ←→ とても難しい<br>1　2　3　4　5　6 |
| | 文法項目 | 過去形（不規則動詞）<br>We swam in the ocean last summer. | |

| | | | とても易しい ←→ とても難しい |
|---|---|---|---|
| 99 | 問 | 東京スカイツリーは東京タワーと同じくらい美しいです。(54)<br>Tokyo Skytree (　　　　　　　　　)<br>Tokyo Tower. | 1　2　3　4　5　6 |
| | 文法項目 | **形容詞の原級による比較**<br>Tokyo Skytree is as beautiful as Tokyo Tower. | |
| 100 | 問 | これが私が30年前住んでいた家です。(92)　※関係副詞を使って<br>This is (　　　　　　　　　　　　　). | 1　2　3　4　5　6 |
| | 文法項目 | **関係副詞（where）**<br>This is the house where I lived 30 years ago. | |
| 101 | 問 | 私はその問題を解決することは簡単だと思いました。(102)　※to不定詞を使って<br>I found (　　　　　) easy (<br>　　　　　　　　　　). | 1　2　3　4　5　6 |
| | 文法項目 | **形式目的語 it（句を伴うもの）**<br>I found it easy to solve the problem. | |
| 102 | 問 | 先生は私たちを早めに家に帰らせてくれました。(89)<br>※使役動詞を使って<br>The teacher (　　　　　　　　　) early. | 1　2　3　4　5　6 |
| | 文法項目 | **原形不定詞**<br>The teacher let us go home early. | |
| 103 | 問 | 新しい自転車を持っていればなあ。(107)<br>I wish (　　　　　　　　) a new bike. | 1　2　3　4　5　6 |
| | 文法項目 | **仮定法過去（I wish ～）**<br>I wish I had a new bike. | |
| 104 | 問 | もし彼女の電話番号を知っていれば，僕は彼女に電話するのに。(106)<br>(　　　　　　　　　) her number, (<br>　　　　　　　　) her. | 1　2　3　4　5　6 |
| | 文法項目 | **仮定法過去**<br>If I knew her number, I would call her. | |
| 105 | 問 | 景気が悪くなると，彼らは仕事を見つけることができませんでした。(98)　※(　)内は3語で<br>When the economy went down, they (<br>　　　　　　　　) jobs. | 1　2　3　4　5　6 |
| | 文法項目 | **助動詞の過去形**<br>When the economy went down, they could not find jobs. | |

| | | | とても易しい ←→ とても難しい |
|---|---|---|---|
| 106 | 問 | 彼女は日本に戻ってくるまで10年間ロンドンに住んでいました。(105) ※（ ）内は4語で<br>She （ ） for 10 years before she came back to Japan. | 1　2　3　4　5　6 |
| | 文法項目 | **過去完了形**<br>She had lived in London for 10 years before she came back to Japan. | |
| 107 | 問 | 私はビルが一人でそこへ行ったのは変だと思いました。(103) ※to不定詞を使わないで<br>I found （ ） strange （ ）. | とても易しい ←→ とても難しい<br>1　2　3　4　5　6 |
| | 文法項目 | **形式目的語 it（節を伴うもの）**<br>I found it strange that Bill went there alone. | |
| 108 | 問 | 彼は私たちに信頼が大切である理由を教えようとしています。(94) ※関係副詞を使って<br>He tries to tell us （ ）. | とても易しい ←→ とても難しい<br>1　2　3　4　5　6 |
| | 文法項目 | **関係副詞（why）**<br>He tries to tell us the reason why trust is important. | |
| 109 | 問 | 天気がいいと，富士山は新宿から見られます。(99)<br>In clear weather, Mt. Fuji （ ） from Shinjuku. | とても易しい ←→ とても難しい<br>1　2　3　4　5　6 |
| | 文法項目 | **助動詞を含む受け身表現**<br>In clear weather, Mt. Fuji can be seen from Shinjuku. | |
| 110 | 問 | 私は私たちが初めて会った日を覚えています。(93)<br>※関係副詞を使って<br>I remember （ ）. | とても易しい ←→ とても難しい<br>1　2　3　4　5　6 |
| | 文法項目 | **関係副詞（when）**<br>I remember the day when we first met. | |

ご協力いただき，まことにありがとうございました。

注）「問」欄にあるカッコの数字は，本書 Table 1.2 の「No.」欄の番号となります。

# Appendix C

## Grammar test for high school students

# 文法テスト1

学籍番号：＿＿＿＿＿＿＿＿＿＿＿

名　　前：＿＿＿＿＿＿＿＿＿＿＿

（問）　日本語の意味に合うよう（　）内の語句を並べ替え，文を完成させなさい。
　　　　また，それぞれの問題が易しいと感じたか，難しいと感じたか，あてはまる
　番号を○で囲みなさい。

　　注意）①選択肢としてカンマ（, ）のみが記されていることもある。
　　　　　②文頭にくる語も小文字にしてある。

| | | |
|---|---|---|
| 1 | 今朝朝食に何を食べましたか。<br>(you / for breakfast / did / this morning / have / what)? | とても易しい ←→ とても難しい<br>1　2　3　4　5　6 |
| 2 | 彼女は和食と中華料理のどちらが好きですか。<br>(like / or / does / Chinese food / she / Japanese food)? | とても易しい ←→ とても難しい<br>1　2　3　4　5　6 |
| 3 | これがあなたの教室ですか。<br>(your classroom / this / is)? | とても易しい ←→ とても難しい<br>1　2　3　4　5　6 |
| 4 | 今日の午後，先生が家に来ます。<br>(to my house / this afternoon / my teacher / will come). | とても易しい ←→ とても難しい<br>1　2　3　4　5　6 |
| 5 | 雨が降った時には彼はバスで図書館へ行きます。<br>(goes / he / by bus / when it rains / to the library). | とても易しい ←→ とても難しい<br>1　2　3　4　5　6 |
| 6 | 彼は一生懸命英語を勉強しています。<br>(very hard / studies / English / he). | とても易しい ←→ とても難しい<br>1　2　3　4　5　6 |

| 7 | ビルは3匹の猫を飼っています。<br>(three cats / Bill / has). | とても易しい ←→ とても難しい<br>1  2  3  4  5  6 |
|---|---|---|
| 8 | 私たちは彼女が病気だと知りませんでした。<br>(was / that / we / ill / didn't / she / know). | とても易しい ←→ とても難しい<br>1  2  3  4  5  6 |
| 9 | 彼女にそのことを教えてあげるわ。<br>(that / will show / her / I). | とても易しい ←→ とても難しい<br>1  2  3  4  5  6 |
| 10 | トムはスーパーへ行き，彼の妻は家にいました。<br>(his wife / Tom / stayed /, / went / home / and / to the supermarket). | とても易しい ←→ とても難しい<br>1  2  3  4  5  6 |
| 11 | 彼は医者になりたいと願っていました。<br>(be / hoped / he / to / a doctor). | とても易しい ←→ とても難しい<br>1  2  3  4  5  6 |
| 12 | 学校まで歩いて通っているのですか。<br>(to school / you / do / walk)? | とても易しい ←→ とても難しい<br>1  2  3  4  5  6 |
| 13 | ここで走ってはいけません。<br>(run / don't / here). | とても易しい ←→ とても難しい<br>1  2  3  4  5  6 |
| 14 | あなたはこの部屋をきれいにしておくべきです。<br>(this room / you / clean / should keep). | とても易しい ←→ とても難しい<br>1  2  3  4  5  6 |
| 15 | こちらが私の先生です。<br>(is / my teacher / this). | とても易しい ←→ とても難しい<br>1  2  3  4  5  6 |
| 16 | 優子は昨日彼と会いました。<br>(him / yesterday / met / Yuko). | とても易しい ←→ とても難しい<br>1  2  3  4  5  6 |

| 17 | ゆっくり歩いてください。<br>(slowly, / please / walk). | とても易しい ←→ とても難しい<br>1  2  3  4  5  6 |
|---|---|---|
| 18 | 私が英語を理解するのは簡単なことではありません。<br>(for me / English / to / it / easy / is / understand / not). | とても易しい ←→ とても難しい<br>1  2  3  4  5  6 |
| 19 | そのジャケット，似合っているよ。<br>(nice / you / in that jacket / look). | とても易しい ←→ とても難しい<br>1  2  3  4  5  6 |
| 20 | 祖父はコンピューターの使い方を知っています。<br>(knows / how / the computer / my grandfather / use / to). | とても易しい ←→ とても難しい<br>1  2  3  4  5  6 |
| 21 | 絵美は野球が好きではありません。<br>(like / Emi / doesn't / baseball). | とても易しい ←→ とても難しい<br>1  2  3  4  5  6 |
| 22 | 机の上のペンは私のです。<br>(mine / on the desk / is / the pen). | とても易しい ←→ とても難しい<br>1  2  3  4  5  6 |
| 23 | 健二，静かにして。<br>(please / Kenji / quiet, / be). | とても易しい ←→ とても難しい<br>1  2  3  4  5  6 |
| 24 | この試合はわくわくします。<br>(exciting / this game / is). | とても易しい ←→ とても難しい<br>1  2  3  4  5  6 |
| 25 | その少女はピアニストになりました。<br>(became / the girl / a pianist). | とても易しい ←→ とても難しい<br>1  2  3  4  5  6 |

| 26 | 彼にメールの送り方を教えてあげました。<br>(how / I / e-mail / him / to / taught / send). | とても易しい ⟷ とても難しい<br>1　2　3　4　5　6 |
|---|---|---|
| 27 | メアリーはあなたにこのチョコレートを食べてほしいと思っています。<br>(you / this chocolate / to / Mary / eat / wants). | とても易しい ⟷ とても難しい<br>1　2　3　4　5　6 |
| 28 | 私の家の前には古い木があります。<br>(is / in front of / there / my house / an old tree). | とても易しい ⟷ とても難しい<br>1　2　3　4　5　6 |
| 29 | えりか，うるさくしないで。<br>(be / don't / noisy, / Erika). | とても易しい ⟷ とても難しい<br>1　2　3　4　5　6 |
| 30 | 先生は私たちに面白い話をしてくれました。<br>(us / the teacher / an interesting story / told). | とても易しい ⟷ とても難しい<br>1　2　3　4　5　6 |
| 31 | 雨が降っていたので外には出ませんでした。<br>(go out / because / I / it / didn't / was raining). | とても易しい ⟷ とても難しい<br>1　2　3　4　5　6 |
| 32 | 私たちは彼を健と呼んでいます。<br>(him / we / Ken / call). | とても易しい ⟷ とても難しい<br>1　2　3　4　5　6 |
| 33 | 私たちは給食を食べるのが好きです。<br>(eating / the school lunch / like / we). | とても易しい ⟷ とても難しい<br>1　2　3　4　5　6 |
| 34 | 私は彼が次に何をするか分かりません。<br>(will do / I / what / next / don't / he / know). | とても易しい ⟷ とても難しい<br>1　2　3　4　5　6 |

# 文法テスト2

学籍番号：＿＿＿＿＿＿＿＿＿＿

名　　前：＿＿＿＿＿＿＿＿＿＿

（問）　日本語の意味に合うよう，（　）に語句を補い，文を完成させなさい。
　　　また，それぞれの問題が易しいと感じたか，難しいと感じたか，あてはまる
　番号を○で囲みなさい。

注意）①カンマ（,）が必要な場合はカンマも含めて記入すること。
　　　②（　）内に入る語は1語とは限らない。

| | | |
|---|---|---|
| 1 | 私はあなたの両親をスーパーで見かけ，トムは彼らを駅で見かけました。<br><br>（　　　　　　　　　　　　　　） at the supermarket, and（<br>　　　　　　　　　　　） at the station. | とても易しい ←→ とても難しい<br>1　2　3　4　5　6 |
| 2 | 明日は晴れるでしょう。<br>※（　）内は3語で<br><br>It（　　　　　　　　　　　　　　　　　） tomorrow. | とても易しい ←→ とても難しい<br>1　2　3　4　5　6 |
| 3 | 私達は今日授業でテレビを見ました。<br><br>We（　　　　　　　　　　　　　　） in class today. | とても易しい ←→ とても難しい<br>1　2　3　4　5　6 |
| 4 | 私の友人の何人かが私の家にやって来ました。<br><br>（　　　　　　　） of（　　　　　　　　　　　） came to my house.<br>　　ここは1語で | とても易しい ←→ とても難しい<br>1　2　3　4　5　6 |
| 5 | 私はこのゲームを20回以上やったことがあります。<br><br>I（　　　　　　　　　　　　　　　　　） more than twenty times. | とても易しい ←→ とても難しい<br>1　2　3　4　5　6 |
| 6 | ナンシーは彼女の姉と同じくらい速く歩くことができます。<br><br>Nancy can（　　　　　　　　　　　　　） her sister. | とても易しい ←→ とても難しい<br>1　2　3　4　5　6 |
| 7 | 彼らは食料を買うためにスーパーへ行きました。<br>※that節を使わずに<br><br>They went to the supermarket（　　　　　　　　　　）. | とても易しい ←→ とても難しい<br>1　2　3　4　5　6 |

| | | |
|---|---|---|
| 8 | 陽子は日本で一番上手にバイオリンを弾くことができます。<br><br>Yoko can（　　　　　　　　　　　　）in Japan. | とても易しい ←→ とても難しい<br>1　2　3　4　5　6 |
| 9 | この腕時計はあの金色のと同じくらい良いなあ。<br><br>This watch（　　　　　　　　　　　　）that gold one. | とても易しい ←→ とても難しい<br>1　2　3　4　5　6 |
| 10 | 私たちはテニスをして楽しみました。<br>※（　）内は2語で<br>We enjoyed（　　　　　　　　　　　　）. | とても易しい ←→ とても難しい<br>1　2　3　4　5　6 |
| 11 | ボルトは世界で一番速く走ることができます。<br><br>Bolt can（　　　　　　　　　　　　）in the world. | とても易しい ←→ とても難しい<br>1　2　3　4　5　6 |
| 12 | 健は由実よりも背が高いです。<br><br>Ken（　　　　　　　　　　　　）Yumi. | とても易しい ←→ とても難しい<br>1　2　3　4　5　6 |
| 13 | 由実は太郎と同じくらい上手にピアノを弾くことができます。<br><br>Yumi can（　　　　　　　　　　　　）Taro. | とても易しい ←→ とても難しい<br>1　2　3　4　5　6 |
| 14 | この機械はフランスで作られました。<br><br>This machine（　　　　　　　　　　　　）. | とても易しい ←→ とても難しい<br>1　2　3　4　5　6 |
| 15 | 生徒たちはやらなければならない宿題がたくさんありました。<br>※（　）内は3語で<br>The students had a lot of（　　　　　　　　）. | とても易しい ←→ とても難しい<br>1　2　3　4　5　6 |
| 16 | 私の母は電話で話しています。<br><br>My mother（　　　　　　　　　）on the phone. | とても易しい ←→ とても難しい<br>1　2　3　4　5　6 |
| 17 | この絵はあの絵よりも美しいです。<br><br>This picture（　　　　　　　　　　　　）that picture. | とても易しい ←→ とても難しい<br>1　2　3　4　5　6 |

| 18 | この車はあの赤いのよりも良いなあ。 | とても易しい ←→ とても難しい 1 2 3 4 5 6 |
| | This car （　　　　　　　　　　） that red one. | |
| 19 | 私たちは毎朝公園を散歩します。 | とても易しい ←→ とても難しい 1 2 3 4 5 6 |
| | We （　　　　　　　　　　　　） every morning. | |
| 20 | 私たちは疲れていて，眠いです。 | とても易しい ←→ とても難しい 1 2 3 4 5 6 |
| | We （　　　　　　　　　　）. | |
| 21 | 由紀は大きくて美しい目をした人形を買いました。 ※関係代名詞を使って | とても易しい ←→ とても難しい 1 2 3 4 5 6 |
| | Yuki bought （　　　　　　　　） large beautiful eyes. | |
| 22 | これが私の一番好きな犬です。 ※関係代名詞を使って | とても易しい ←→ とても難しい 1 2 3 4 5 6 |
| | This is （　　　　　　　　　　） the best. | |
| 23 | 彼はロンドンに2年間住んでいます。 ※（　）内は4語で | とても易しい ←→ とても難しい 1 2 3 4 5 6 |
| | He （　　　　　　　　　） for two years. | |
| 24 | これは私のカバンですが，あのカバンはあなたのです。 | とても易しい ←→ とても難しい 1 2 3 4 5 6 |
| | （　　　　　　　）, but that one is （　　　　　）. | |
| 25 | ジョンはクラスで一番背が高い少年です。 | とても易しい ←→ とても難しい 1 2 3 4 5 6 |
| | John （　　　　　　　　） boy in the class. | |
| 26 | あの寝ている赤ちゃんを見てください。 | とても易しい ←→ とても難しい 1 2 3 4 5 6 |
| | Look at that （　　　　　　　　）. | |
| 27 | ジミーは彼の兄よりも速く泳ぐことができます。 | とても易しい ←→ とても難しい 1 2 3 4 5 6 |
| | Jimmy can （　　　　　　　　） his brother. | |

| 28 | 富士山は日本で一番美しい山です。<br><br>Mt. Fuji ( ) mountain in Japan. | とても易しい ←→ とても難しい<br>1　2　3　4　5　6 |
|---|---|---|
| 29 | 柔道は世界の多くの人々によって楽しまれています。<br><br>Judo ( ) in the world. | とても易しい ←→ とても難しい<br>1　2　3　4　5　6 |
| 30 | 私は将来の仕事で英語を使いたいです。<br><br>I want ( ) in my future job. | とても易しい ←→ とても難しい<br>1　2　3　4　5　6 |
| 31 | これはこの店で一番良いカメラです。<br><br>This ( ) in this store. | とても易しい ←→ とても難しい<br>1　2　3　4　5　6 |
| 32 | 私はジョンと同じくらい背が高いです。<br><br>I ( ) John. | とても易しい ←→ とても難しい<br>1　2　3　4　5　6 |
| 33 | 彼は家族の中で一番ゆっくり食べます。<br><br>He ( ) in my family. | とても易しい ←→ とても難しい<br>1　2　3　4　5　6 |
| 34 | 彼は彼の父と同じくらいゆっくり運転します。<br><br>He ( ) his father. | とても易しい ←→ とても難しい<br>1　2　3　4　5　6 |
| 35 | 私はちょうど自分の部屋を掃除したところです。<br><br>I ( ). | とても易しい ←→ とても難しい<br>1　2　3　4　5　6 |
| 36 | 彼は去年中国にいました。<br><br>He ( ) last year. | とても易しい ←→ とても難しい<br>1　2　3　4　5　6 |
| 37 | これは多くの学生によって読まれている本です。<br>※関係代名詞を使わずに<br><br>This is a book ( ). | とても易しい ←→ とても難しい<br>1　2　3　4　5　6 |

| 38 | 次郎は花子よりもゆっくり話します。 <br><br> Jiro（　　　　　　　　　　　　　）Hanako. | とても易しい ←→ とても難しい <br> 1　2　3　4　5　6 |
|---|---|---|
| 39 | 私は赤よりも青が好きです。 <br><br> I like（　　　　　　　　　　　）red. | とても易しい ←→ とても難しい <br> 1　2　3　4　5　6 |
| 40 | 私はその時本を読んでいました。 <br><br> I（　　　　　　　　　　　　　）then. | とても易しい ←→ とても難しい <br> 1　2　3　4　5　6 |
| 41 | 私たちは去年の夏に海で泳ぎました。 <br><br> We（　　　　　　　　　　）last summer. | とても易しい ←→ とても難しい <br> 1　2　3　4　5　6 |
| 42 | 東京スカイツリーは東京タワーと同じくらい美しいです。 <br><br> Tokyo Skytree（　　　　　　　　　）Tokyo Tower. | とても易しい ←→ とても難しい <br> 1　2　3　4　5　6 |

**Taeko Kamimura** teaches EFL composition and applied linguistics at Senshu University in Japan. She received a Ph.D. in English at Indiana University of Pennsylvania in the USA.

She has published various books and articles on EFL writing, including *Teaching EFL Composition in Japan* (Senshu University Press), *A Handbook for Writers of Essays and Research Papers* (coauthored with Kyoko Oi, Kenkyusha), "Composing Summaries of a Narrative Story Produced under Different Conditions" (*Journal of Pan-Pacific Association of Applied Linguistics*), and "The Effects of Integrated EFL Instruction on Japanese EFL Students' Ability to Produce Argumentative Writing" (*KATE Journal*). She is also one of the authors of university English writing textbooks *Writing Power* (Kenkyusha) and *Writing Frontiers* as well as high school writing textbooks *Word Trek* (Kiriharashoten) and *Empower English Expression I and II* (Kiriharashoten).

本書は令和元年度専修大学図書刊行助成を受けて出版するものであり，科学研究費補助金（基盤研究（C），課題番号 15K02698）の援助を受けて行われた研究が基となっている。

### EFL Grammar for Japanese Students and Teachers

2020 年 1 月 20 日　初版 1 刷発行

著　者　Taeko Kamimura

発行者　上原伸二

発行所　専修大学出版局
　　　　〒101-0051 東京都千代田区神田神保町 3-10-3
　　　　　　　　　　（株）専大センチュリー内
　　　　03-3263-4230（代）

印刷・製本　株式会社　加藤文明社

装幀　尾崎美千子

ISBN978-4-88125-341-0

Printed in Japan.